*For Kathy,
who has be
for the long, long ~~name~~.
in appreciation of our
friendship!*

xox

The Next You

Discovering Confidence, Calm, and Courage—*Now*

by **Posy Gering**

Trebay Press
Seattle, WA
2013

978-0-9910734-0-5   Print

978-0-9910734-1-2   Amazon/kindle

Cover design by Leslie Waltzer
Interior book design by Kristi Ryder

For information about special discounts for bulk purchases, to bring Posy Gering to speak at your live event, and for copyright permission, please contact (206) 769-9465 or *nextu@mynextu.com*.

This book is dedicated to June Ekman,
source, mentor, mother and friend.

Table of Contents

Introduction

We all want to be satisfied with our lives and happy in our choices. Consider how much time, energy, and money we invest to ensure our roads take us to those ends. But sometimes, in spite of our best efforts, we find ourselves at a standstill and we have to ask, "What is keeping me from enjoying life to its fullest?"

Perhaps you can identify with answers like:

> *I find myself stuck in some vicious cycle*
>
> *I believe I never quite measure up*
>
> *I feel tense or tied up in knots*
>
> *I believe I'm a fraud*
>
> *I feel that life has knocked me down and I can't get up*
>
> *I'll enjoy my life when I lose weight, make more money, have the right job or mate, etc.*
>
> *I lack the courage, confidence, or spark to step out of the wrong path and into the right path*

Perhaps it might be something else. Whatever your answer, it probably seems very real, unquestionably true, and utterly inescapable.

You're not alone. You aren't the only one who feels stuck in low-grade unhappiness and dissatisfaction. Whatever your situation is, it is within your power to experience more of the great possibilities that life has to offer. At any moment, you can uncover unrecognized strengths and liberate unseen resources to deal with life's challenges. Break away from those chains starting now.

Within this book I will teach you how to escape the clutches of the thing that is holding you back. You'll find these pages chock-full of secrets that allow you to break through those concrete truths so that you can begin to restore and more fully experience calm, confidence, courage, and other qualities more broadly known as happiness, no matter what is happening internally or externally. You will have more of the life you want.

This book offers a proven methodology, called *NextU*, that breaks through the habitual barriers that keep you from possibility, confidence, and peace of mind. This methodology is based on recent findings from a wide range of disciplines: cognitive science and ancient wisdom, creative process and biology, human development, and improvisation.

The method is called *NextU*, a deliberate play on the concepts "next you" and "next university." I chose it because it implies aspiration and learning, both of which are required to get to your next desired state of being. This method teaches you how to free yourself from your habitual, automatic responses, so that you can experience the confidence, calm, and courage you've longed for. The *NextU* method invites you to focus on very small essential units, just as if you were learning a new dance. In order to get to the next you, you'll need *NextU*.

You'll first be introduced to my *NextU* method, followed by step-by-step applications for specific common situations. These exercises help you play with the wiring of your automatic ways of being so that you experience the spark that might be possible if you had an alternative. They teach you how to intervene in the automatic cycles that keep you stuck, and show you how to build new awareness, skills, and capacity for the life you want.

The absence of possibility holds you back

NextU proposes that the biggest thing holding you back is your perception of what's possible, but just telling you to increase your perception is not especially helpful. What is helpful is to look at what produces this sense. Your awareness of possibility is one of the products of your perception.

Perception is the way you understand and interpret the world. Your perception is made up of what is going on in your mind and your body. In your mind, your perception comprises what you notice, the conclusions you arrive at, and what you assume, believe, and feel. It is all the factors that add up to what you believe is real and true.

Your body influences your perception as well. You've probably experienced tension of your muscles, restriction of your breath, or adrenaline or other hormones racing through your system. Most likely, you can also recall visceral sensations of great pleasure. These are just a few examples of how you interact with your body's sensory systems.

Together your mind and body are integrating, regulating, and communicating through many systems that all provide information to you that you're largely unconscious of, but that nonetheless contribute to how you see the world.

The reason these factors are so effective at holding you back is that you consider them to be "real" or "true." Investing in the truth of what you perceive is what is called sanity. For example, you know that if you run into a wall, the wall will stop you. You will fall down and be hurt.

However, there is an untold story about your grip on reality. It tends to lock you into a limited set of possibilities. This is the dark shadow of your evolutionary success. While your perception happens effectively and instantaneously, at the famous speed of thought, your newly formulated sense of truth excludes the chance of any other possibility and reinforces your current belief. While this is valuable if your actions in the next moment affect your survival, it becomes difficult to imagine or act for a different outcome.

Because of this extremely well-developed evolutionary capacity we all have for perceiving reality, **NextU** offers a different, pleasantly subversive route. Instead of trying to change your belief, **NextU** helps you utilize your other senses and systems so that you can feel your way into new territory full of possibility.

Try it now

Remember smelling some wonderful scent. Perhaps it surrounded you as you walked out of your door; perhaps it was a smell that told you that you were home or that it had finally rained.

Give yourself a moment to relish and recreate the memory.

Notice what just happened and how you feel now.

You probably recalled a very specific memory.

As you remembered, you probably took a deep, full breath and sighed without even thinking about it. You may even feel a desire to take another deep breath.

How did that make you feel? Clearer? Calmer? Better? That shift, whether momentary or lasting, is evidence that you changed your perception.

This is an example of what you'll find in this book. The core of this book is organized around a variety of specific barriers that hold you back and unusual ways to leave them behind. The barriers are very familiar. They show up all the time in the guise of your favorite limiting thoughts.

Change the songs on your internal playlist

Pause for a minute and sample what's going on in your mind. There is a pretty steady stream of thoughts covering a range of things like noticing physical sensations, going over something someone said or did to you, judging yourself, another person or a situation, anticipating what you or another person will say or do, making a list of things you don't want to forget, losing track of the idea that you were supposed to pay attention to, musing on all thing things you should have, would have, could have done, and a million more.

It's likely that there's a refrain—some thought measuring or evaluating yourself in some way that plays over and over. In the *NextU* method they are called limiting thoughts because your belief in them is so strong you cannot imagine anything different when you are in their clutches. If you look at the list of limiting thoughts at the beginning of Chapter 4, you will see examples of the most common refrains. This is not to imply that you should only have positive thoughts.

Limits are a gift, because they define the edges of your experience that tell you where growth is needed; instead of free-floating anxiety or undifferentiated fog, limits provide shape and specificity. When you become aware of one of these thoughts, it is as if you get a handle that opens a secret door.

Unfortunately, if you are like most people, you believe you can punish, berate, or shame yourself in to better behavior. This kind of belief hammers away at your confidence, calm, and courage, keeping you in a self-constructed jail. This is an ineffective strategy if what you desire from better behavior is more love, happiness, or self-acceptance.

NextU introduces alternative strategies designed to support the amazing, creative, lovable human being that you are and to help you experience the pleasure, possibility, and wonder of life. What differentiates *NextU* from other methods is that it does not just give advice; rather, it recognizes that from where you stand now you cannot get to where you want without the right tools. *NextU* is about making the crossing.

How to bridge the gap

This book is subtitled *"Discovering confidence, calm, and courage now."* It implies that your state of mind right now is not satisfying and there is a gap between where you are right now and those qualities you long for. It is easy to gloss over how difficult it is to bridge the gap from here to there. Without understanding what is behind the scenes, it often seems as insignificant as the space between a period and the beginning of a new sentence.

This metaphor is more apt than most. In grammar, a period indicates the end of a thought, and the new sentence begins a new discrete idea. That shift from one idea to the next means verbs are involved. In real-life application, bridging that gap means you have to do something. Perhaps you once stood at the edge of a high dive or on a log over a rushing stream, and you froze. Other people's advice or encouragement did little to quell your fear. Perhaps shame got you moving or you turned back or someone helped you.

Exhortations like *"Just do it!"* prevent you from paying attention to what you really need and from taking the critical steps that lead to a different experience. But there is an alternative, one where you feel filled with the courage to change your situation, the inspiration to believe and act, and the power to break down the barriers and ask for help.

This book is organized around those three themes: inspiration, intervention, and breakthrough. Here are some ways that **NextU** defines inspiration, intervention, and breakthrough, as well as an invitation for you to think about what they mean to you.

Inspiration is your endlessly renewable beginning.

- Your spark of belief.
- Your fuel for renewal.
- Your awe of nature's daily miracles.
- Your trust in possibility.
- Your recovery of innocence.

Intervention is acting in the moment on your behalf.

- It provides the nudge for an unambiguous "no."
- It holds you steady when you feel like giving up.

- It redraws your boundaries.
- It dusts you off when you stumble.
- It refuses to accept a lie.

Breakthrough removes the barriers.
- You drop the baggage of the past.
- You get out of jail free.
- You shed your too-confining skin.
- You enter a new level.
- You taste the forbidden, with a touch of mischief.

Exploring your meaning of important words is a powerful tool that enables change. Take a moment and consider:

What does inspiration mean to you?

What might inspiration spark in you?

What does intervention mean to you?

Which pattern needs to be interrupted?

What does breakthrough mean to you?

What barrier are you longing to break through?

Why I wrote this book

I wrote this book because I've filled a tool chest with effective ways to recover, refocus, re-energize, and renew myself. I use these tools all the time. Every day there are endless opportunities to get stuck in a traffic jam of negativity or frustration, be flattened by disappointment, or feel over-stretched or squeezed in order to fit what I believe are other people's expectations of me. These are just a few types of challenging moments you may identify with. In these moments it's easy to be blinded to the possibility of starting over.

I have shared these tools and techniques with hundreds of clients and students. Their results validated my personal experience that *NextU* provides a practical way to escape the clutches of the thoughts holding you back and can shift your perception of what is possible. I wrote this book to share these techniques even more widely.

These tools are distilled from over forty years of study and practice. The main influences have been Remy Charlip and Shirley Kaplan's work on creative process, and June Ekman's mentoring informed by Alexander Technique, Orgonomy, somatic techniques, meditation, dance, visual and performing arts. I hold a master's degree in organizational development, which included in-depth explorations of subjects like leadership, whole systems thinking, cognitive and neuroscience, adult learning theory, design thinking, and personal mastery. In addition, generous teachers—change theorists, spiritual teachers, biologists, artists, writers, and questioners—continue to shape and inform my work.

I created these practices from necessity, as I climbed out and tried to stay out of the black hole left as a result of childhood sexual and emotional abuse. While good psychotherapy provided the heavy lifting and developed a healthy foundation, I had to develop proficiency in day-to-day resilience.

These tools help clean up the wreckage of the past, as represented by your thought patterns, and amplify the experiences of aliveness. Aliveness means experiencing the wonder and range of life, such as vibrancy, creativity, energy, awe, appreciation, authenticity, and awareness of the miracle that life and consciousness is. My intention is to share my secrets, so you can increase your pleasure, love, and awestruck wonder, too.

How this book is organized

This book has five sections:

- *Chapter 1* explains the *NextU* theory and method.

- *Chapter 2* takes a close look at three catalysts: intervention, inspiration, and breakthrough and why they are necessary for lasting change.

- *Chapter 3* clarifies the foundation used in the *NextU* exercises.

- *Chapter 4* contains examples of limiting thoughts and short one-minute exercises on how to break through them.

- And *Chapter 5* presents frequently asked questions, some concluding thoughts, and a more in-depth explanation of why I chose to write this book.

In *Chapter 1*, you will learn about the scientific theories and concepts informing the *NextU* method. In extremely brief form, the method is built on three premises: utilize mind and body, expand perceptual awareness, and scale expectations of success to the smallest increments. This creates small, organic, shifts in the moment that give you keys to large and lasting effects. However, you do not need to understand the theory to benefit from the practices. You can skip right to the exercises in Chapter 4.

Chapter 2 discusses these limiting thoughts in relation to the three themes that broadly represent what change is needed most now: intervention, inspiration, or breakthrough. You can use the theme as a lens to focus your practice.

In Chapter 3, *Foundations*, you'll learn how to get the most out of the exercises by preparing your physical, intellectual and neurological space. These foundations are powerful practices on their own that can help you navigate stressful situations at a lower cost to your psyche, body, and spirit.

Chapter 4 contains the actual exercises based around mundane limiting thoughts. A suggested treatment called a "one-minute transformation" for each of those limiting thoughts follows. You will find a very short explanation of how each remedy was discovered, as well as step-by-step directions for applying the remedy yourself. These remedies can be construed as exercises because they tell you what to do, as meditations because they prescribe quieting your body and focusing your mind, or as interventions because they interrupt your usual way of doing things.

You will get even more out of the book if you take a few moments and reflect on your experience of each exercise. To that end, you'll find a few guiding reflection questions. The questions help you do research on yourself by honing your sensory awareness and learning how to translate the language of your experience. If you are willing to record what you notice, you will be able to identify patterns and successes, and make connections about the effects of interrupting habits. The more you increase your awareness of its impact on you, the more you can choose how to respond to disruptions in the future.

In **Chapter 5** you'll find your own "owner's manual" where you'll learn more about my background, find answers to some frequently asked questions, find some helpful applications for complex situations, and get a few final concluding thoughts.

NextU worked for me. It has worked for hundreds of others. Now, you can use it too.

CHAPTER 1

NextU Theory and Method

NextU theory

The theory behind *NextU* is based in a principle of Euclidean geometry: An infinite number of lines can pass through any given point. That suggests that at any point in life, there is an infinite number of possibilities. The challenge is that you usually see only one or two.

The words most often used to describe those one or two options are usually pretty loaded terms, such as good or bad, right or wrong, success or failure—and they sound limited and factual. It is the nature of our brains to respond to what we perceive is "really" there and to solve problems that appear before us. We fight, flee, or fix. While these instincts give us an incredible evolutionary advantage, they affect what we perceive as possible, eliminating the other 99.9 percent that might be.

While you may judge many of those infinite options as ridiculous, impractical, or impossible, stirring up your brain is a necessary activity to get to something different. Albert Einstein said, "We can't solve problems by using the same kind of thinking we used when we created them." This book will help you find those other possibilities and expand your repertoire of thinking.

One big delusion about happiness is that once you achieve it, you are there forever—that it is a steady state. You only need to remember the last time you were driving on a beautiful day and someone cut you off to know how quickly life intervenes, setting off an automatic chain reaction that shatters your peace of mind. It is natural. These things happen all the time. The secret is in changing how you recover.

Your gateway of perception

The definition of recovery includes the concept of return, regaining, getting back. You are not chasing something out of reach; rather, you already possess the alternatives, abilities, and awareness. They just have gotten buried in a lifetime of habits that served you at one time, but limit you now.

Recovery involves overcoming or letting go of the thing that is holding you back. *NextU* proposes that the major thing holding you back is your perception, the way you understand your world. There are two main reasons why it is hard to change your perception: first, the word "perception" is usually synonymous with "the truth" in your mind; secondly, perception is more like a hydra, the many-headed monster that was slain by Hercules, than like a single, discrete thing.

Your brain is the result of millions of years of successful evolution. One huge advantage the brain developed early on was the ability to deal with stimuli extremely quickly, predicting and reacting to threats, and mobilizing to get away or to get dinner. Although this behavior contributed to biological success, generally, these reactions do not produce the relationships or peace of mind you want.

The brain manages a phenomenal amount of thoughts, sensations, memories, external stimuli, and feedback from other systems. It selects, filters, and reinforces what is going on externally and combines it with what is going on internally, to create your awareness or consciousness.

Your consciousness is the way you make sense of, interpret, represent, or model the world we experience. It is also how we make predictions about that world. For example, it helps keep you from tripping on the stairs, plan for dinner, and keep track of your keys. Most of the time, what you are aware of defines what is real and true. However, real and true for you is not necessarily the same for others.

Here are two common examples:

- ▶ Think of a time when you had a disagreement with a partner, child, sibling, or someone close to you. Chances are that somewhere in that disagreement each of you believed you were right, and you each insisted that the other see things the same way as you.

- ▶ Remember a time when someone was late and you were very angry. Then you later learned that your friend or partner was late because he or she had to deal with some very difficult life situation. You may remember the indignation, the vicious cycle of thoughts, and something along the lines of "How could he..." while you were waiting. Then, when you learned about the circumstances, a huge release of tension and emotion drained out of you. Your feelings of blame may have shifted to feelings of compassion.

While this may or may not accurately describe your situation, it illustrates how a change in perception changes your feelings and viewpoint.

Admittedly, this is an extremely simplistic and superficial discussion of perception. The point is there is no single truth internally or externally. If you do not like the results you are getting from your life, this is great news because it means that many more realities are available to you with a shift in your perception.

The challenge is the strong conviction that you are right. When you feel this way, it's very difficult to believe in anything else. That is where *NextU* comes in. *NextU* gives you the secrets to liberate more of yourself. It integrates a mind-body approach, increases access to your innate tools for taking in and interpreting the world, and radically changes the scale of your perception.

The *NextU* method

Integrate mind and body. Tap your senses. Scale down to a moment.

A holistic, mind-body approach is at the heart of the *NextU* approach. Western science limits knowing and innovation to a very small portion of the brain—the rational, thinking portion. The *NextU* method includes the whole of you, helping you take advantage of your other elegant, highly sophisticated systems. These systems sense, monitor, receive, send, and interpret your interactions with the world as a biological entity. Western culture generally trains you to disconnect and ignore signals from your own systems, in favor of adopting perceptions and ways of thinking portrayed in the media and science.

The *NextU* method shows you how to receive these frequently ignored systems and base your actions more on their input. The secret of utilizing them is to get your intellect out of the way. This dominating brain function deserves respect, as it has given you a huge amount of success so far in your life. However, the reason you want to get around your intellect is because it's only going to tell you what you know, which keeps you firmly rooted in repeating the past.

Some people are able to tell themselves to think differently, and that works. Most people, perhaps including you, find themselves sucked back into some vicious cycle. Luckily, there is more than your intellect at play. Your senses, nervous system, breath, emotion, musculature, and imagination can be tapped to circumvent or breakthrough what limits you.

In many popular action movies some unstoppable monster or weapon threatens survival. The hero manages to change some of the inner controls of the monster or weapon, rendering it harmless or making it self-destruct. This book will give you a similar power in your own life. You will be able to get inside the things that are holding you back, play with some of the controls, and discover a better outcome.

This is not to suggest that your usual way of believing is monstrous—rather, that it is very powerful and appears unstoppable. That is why you need some slightly subversive strategies. Instead of hammering away at trying to change your intellect, which is like a highly fortified front door, look for alternatives by finding the back door, which in this metaphor is akin to using different senses.

The third premise of *NextU* is to shrink the scale of what you are trying to change. Just like research, you will need to identify what you are going to study, experiment with, and measure. Instead of trying to change your whole life, scale it down: one thought, instead of everything. Right now, instead of always.

While this sounds simplistic, when compared to the overwhelming life situation you are facing, it becomes clear why its simplicity is deliberate. Working with a very small unit has unique advantages. It helps you parse the complexity so that you can find a starting point, take action, notice the effects of your choice, and decide whether you want to continue. The small scale also means an effective intervention takes only a minute or two.

To get to "Wow!" step into now

When was the last time you felt you were living right now? It's a paradox: The only time you can really live or change is the present moment, yet it's incredibly difficult to get your mind and body to fully be in that moment. Most of the time the mind is preoccupied with reliving the past or anticipating the future, neither of which you can do anything about. Scientists, spiritual teachers, artists, and athletes agree that the most pleasure, serenity, and flow occur when you are in the present—and getting there takes practice.

The good news is that as long as you're alive you have countless opportunities to experiment with alternative methods of perceiving, collecting data, and evaluating the effects. The more you practice even partial seconds of self-acceptance, satisfaction, and success, the better you become at noticing and enjoying these moments or recognizing that you are not experiencing them and recovering.

While a second of experience compared to a lifetime of

deeply ingrained habits may seem like trying to move the ocean with a teaspoon, each time you have a new experience, it's significant. If you can free yourself once, you can do it again. If you can do it twice, you can start stringing these little pearls together. As soon as you recognize that you have fallen into the clutches of your favorite way of holding yourself back, which may happen immediately, you can practice repeatedly intervening in order to experience an alternative.

The *NextU* meditations do not result in "happily ever after." Instead they give you a set of tools along with instructions on how to have the freedom to choose more aliveness in the present moment. Aliveness is an umbrella word for peace of mind, sense of purpose, and other qualities that enhance your joy in being alive. Aliveness spurs courage, confidence, wonder, innocence, and playfulness, to name a few favorites that detail what being more alive is like. *NextU* teaches you how to get back in alignment with these desired qualities when you get derailed.

One of the most popular misconceptions is that happiness or peace of mind or any of the other experiential feelings is a steady state—you either have it or you don't. Perhaps that is true in movies or fairy tales, but in life, they are dynamic, expanding, contracting, shifting, or being shifted all the time. It's like balancing on one foot: Sometimes you do it easily, other times you wobble and fall. If you work on learning to balance better and more predictably, you learn that you have to call on many other support systems besides your foot, including your musculature, proprioception, and skeletal and auditory systems, just to name a few.

All these behind-the-scenes systems are the invisible components helping a ballerina stand elegantly on point.

The same is true of life. A complex pattern of interactions happens below the surface of your consciousness. But only the pain or pleasure, resentment or gratitude, success or disappointment gets your attention. You can view feelings as the only things existing or view them as clues in your ongoing investigation of life.

Fractals of change

In mathematics, fractals are never-ending patterns that are the same at the smallest as well as at the largest scale. This book proposes that your responses to and interpretation of external and internal stimuli are also fractals. They are the same at the micro level and the macro. Your response patterns include neurological, hormonal, intellectual, emotional, physical, autonomic, and spiritual elements and add up to what we call experience or perception.

NextU helps you gain skill in sensing and interpreting more of these dynamics that drive the warp and weft of perception. In some ways, perception is like a kaleidoscope. When you look through the hole, a dazzling pattern appears. The picture seems complete, but if a single bead or fragment moves, the whole pattern shifts.

Subtle changes have big impact. You may have experienced a crying baby who couldn't be comforted until swaddled in a blanket. As an adult, it's hard to swaddle yourself, but other physical practices have a similar effect, like sighing deeply or sitting in a chair with your back against the back of the chair and your feet flat on the floor. These simple actions send neurological signals that it is safe to be in your body, so you can get out of a state of emergency and consider alternative ways of responding.

NextU is not just for emergencies. On the other end of the experience spectrum, think about something exciting you have either experienced or that you can anticipate happening. Notice how even one thought can produce a feeling of more energy, alertness, optimism, and/or a lift in your posture. In addition, you may enjoy the positive feelings even more fully.

NextU helps you learn the language of your patterns so you can play with them. The language composes your experience. To learn this language, you need to recognize that it is happening, acknowledge its validity, and use all of your senses to help translate its meaning.

Why your senses?

Your senses are highly sensitive, automatic data gathering systems. They interact with your brain to give you information about what is going on in and around your body. Then your brain interprets that information. However, this interpretation is closer to what your brain wants to be there than what really is. If you go back to the primary sensory data, you have an opportunity for a very different reading.

Increasingly, there is exciting scientific research that informs these ideas. In Scientific American, MacNeilage, Rogers, and Vallortigara published research about the evolutionary origins of the right and left brain. They claimed that our brains and bodies are the living proof of billions of years of successful evolution, and that humans survived and thrived because they could respond both instantaneously and creatively. But they found that one thing that gave humans a huge advantage— more than just responding in the moment—was being able to predict, take meaning from, and make life-supportive decisions around their environmental data, such as sounds, footprints, and smells. This is primarily the work of your left brain.

The problem for most of us is that the left brain is dominant. While jumping to conclusions is an amazing capacity, you may have discovered its limits, such as in your relationships. Your brain is amazing; it works at lightning speed. That means that you arrive at conclusions or react instantly. Think back to the last time you got angry. You might remember noticing automatic changes in your muscles, breathing, heart rate, perspiration, ability to sleep, or digestion, to name a few physical changes.

The left-brain's dominance also shows up in the content, volume, and persistence of certain thoughts. The left brain draws from the past and tries to anticipate the future. You might notice you seem to spend a lot of time going over something that happened in the past or worrying about the future. That's just your left brain doing its very best for you. It may not stop providing its flood of thoughts, but you can change your relationship to it, sidestepping its force or surfing the surface.

The good news is that you're also wired to be able to do things differently. This ability is another huge evolutionary advantage. Being able to adapt, imagine, create, sense, perceive, and feel: This is your right brain.

This book builds on these two findings, enabling you to intervene when experiencing those automatic habits and uncover or hone alternatives that will help you experience more of the life you really want.

These lessons explain how your innate biology can support changing your experience. The directions include steps that help you become more aware of your physical body, respiration, and emotions so that you tap into alternative sources for relief. These other sources are allies that can help you overcome your knee-jerk reactions to what is going on externally and internally.

Why is it so important to feel?

Think of times when you *knew* what an answer was. Chances are you will say that it felt right or you felt it in your gut. Now, remember a peak experience. Whether it was riding a roller coaster, reaching a once-daunting milestone, or achieving a physical feat, it had a very definite set of sensations.

In fact, if you think of the times when you were most satisfied, it's likely that you associate feelings such as pleasure, accomplishment, or connection with the experience. These are sensations that you feel viscerally. And you are more likely to experience them more when you are aware of or connected to what you are experiencing in the moment. This connection between inner awareness and sensation and outer stimulus is what is commonly called being present in your life.

When you're more present, you're open to more possibility. This book shows you ways to connect with your whole self, so you can mine the amazing and renewable resources that give you confidence, courage, serenity, or whatever quality you seek. The challenge is that when you explore your resources more deeply, you may encounter some "B–list" feelings, as well.

Loving the A-list *and* the B-list

I grew up believing that there was an A-list comprised of ideal qualities—the way we're supposed to be—and that there was a definitely inferior B-list. The A-list included qualities like cheerful, happy, positive, cute, loving, generous, and in control of your life. The B-list contained the feelings that were better kept in a closet: resentment, petulance, jealousy, selfishness, insecurity, tension, lack of control, imperfection. I believed we were supposed to exemplify the A- list. The trouble is that the B-list describes more of life than the A-list.

What happens when you are told to "Cheer up" or "Get over it"? Perhaps you balk or pretend. Perhaps such orders make you feel angrier, lonelier, and even more hopeless. This book is for closeted grouches and whiners. Here you can freely admit to your negative, self-limiting defeatist thoughts—and, if you feel like it, experiment with different responses to them.

You may think it would take a SWAT team to bust you out of your habitual way of responding. Yet the opposite is true: All you need is yourself. It's because you mobilize your own resources to break through and uncover your own experience that transformation occurs. This is what authenticity is about: You increase awareness and make choices in alignment with your whole self.

Summary

Now you have an introduction to the theory of *NextU*. The premise is that what's holding you back from enjoying your life is your own perception. *NextU* offers a three-pronged approach to changing your perception by integrating mind and body, treating yourself holistically, and reducing the scale and scope of what you are trying to change down to a single thought. In the next chapter, you'll learn more about the three catalysts to change and about how to get the most out of the exercises.

Chapter 2

The Three Catalysts of the Next You

Intervention, Inspiration, Breakthrough

This chapter looks a little deeper at the drivers of change, what **NextU** calls the three catalysts: intervention, inspiration, and breakthrough, as well as the iceberg that often sinks your efforts.

There are many reasons to change. What drives many individuals is pain, the frustration of hitting the same wall repeatedly, and/or longing. If you want to change, you should ask yourself three basic questions: What do you want to start? What do you need to stop? What stumbling block or wall do you want to avoid?

Your answers need to be specific because you need to know where to focus your efforts and how you're going to evaluate your results. Also, real change is going to involve some level of discomfort or risk. It's always easier to deflect the difficult work of making change to an area of comfort or ease than to step outside your comfort zone. Because most change is outside of your comfort zone, you need some kind of catalyst to start the journey and keep the process more compelling so you don't return to your habitual ways of being.

Think about what keeps you from starting, stopping, or avoiding that thing you just identified. Chances are one of three things is missing. You need to find more mental stimulation to start, something to interfere enough to alter or hinder an action, or a new, clear, and perhaps sudden understanding of the situation.

In Chapter 4 you will find a variety of exercises. As you do each exercise, you might ask yourself what catalyst you need in each instance and apply your results accordingly.

Intervention

What do you need to stop?

How many times have you found yourself in the clutches of a familiar pattern, yet you keep eating those cookies or drinking too much or not getting enough sleep? It's a vicious cycle. You probably have a list of what you "should not" be doing and what you "should" be doing instead. Then, when you don't do what you think you should, you probably deploy the big guns of judgment, disapproval, and self-condemnation.

The only real result you get from this reaction is feeling really bad about yourself. You vow that you'll never do that behavior again, except you do. Mostly, it's a familiar treadmill—going round and round, and you continually find yourself where you started, or even more deeply stuck in that particular rut.

If only there were someone or something that would stop you from taking that first step down the slippery slope! If only there were an escape hatch from the vicious cycle! *NextU* cannot supply a personal enforcement officer or superman to swoop in and save you, but it can do something better. Namely, it teaches you how to take control and get back on course.

The intervention exercises give you the support to stop your limiting thoughts right now. Sometimes all you need is a little nudge. At other times, you may have to meet the strength of the limiting thought with equal energy and volume. Habits are powerful.

Most habits are based in good intentions. Often the habit protects you from having to feel pain, shame, or fear. It's usually so effective that it springs into action without a conscious thought on your part. Fighting habits directly, as you no doubt already know, is difficult.

The difficulty of direct confrontation prompted the development of more subversive approaches in the *NextU* method. The idea is to get beyond the front line of defense, to the soft underbelly of the habit. In this book you will find back door access routes to help you pause and begin a different trajectory that deflects those relentless self-defeating cycles, so that you can start accumulating new successes.

Inspiration

What do you want to start?
Sometimes stopping is not the issue. Rather, getting started in the first place is what's difficult. You might feel a flatness or hopelessness about even trying to change, thinking, "Why bother?"

These moments call for inspiration. It's worth noting that the root of the word inspiration comes from Latin and means "to breathe in." You need ways to pump up your courage and innocence so that you can risk dreaming, find optimism, and discover alternate definitions of success. *NextU* will help you strike the sparks that reignite your flame of inspiration.

You might try conscious breathing right now, just as an experiment. What I mean by conscious breathing is to focus your attention on the rhythms, flow, and qualities of your breath as fully as possible. Observe how your breath and your body affect one another. Feel the air traveling through your entire breathing mechanism–nose, throat, lungs, and belly—as you inhale and exhale. Be gentle. After three or four breaths, allow your breath to return to normal. Notice any differences in the way you feel.

Most people report feeling more alert, awake, energized. Perhaps you can identify. If you're feeling dizzy, slow down and do less. Overachieving in this exercise can definitely knock you off balance. Scale down to a level at which you notice results.

Now notice how you increased your recognition of possibilities. Answers to a problem might seem clearer. What appeared before as a pinhole or a window, might now appear to open wider, letting in the fresh air of new optimism.

Sometimes what prevents a person from starting is a guarantee that he or she will achieve the goal in one try. The secret is that what is called starting is, in reality, not a one-time event. Rather, the key is the ability to start again and again and again for each step, even though the way is uncertain.

Inspiration in this sense is the exercise of clearing away the barnacles of cynicism, hopelessness, baggage, and self-judgment. It is about reclaiming innocence, finding joy in being an eternal beginner, and declaring, "I don't know."

Again, as an experiment, notice what effect reading those last few sentences had on you. Just thinking about something you long for can have an uplifting impact on your body and energy level.

There is a popular saying our culture subscribes to: "When the going gets tough, the tough get going." If and when you agree, you tighten your muscles, clench your jaw, clamp down on your feelings, and push yourself through no matter what.

NextU counters that when the going gets tough, it's time to soften, increase compassion, and listen. It calls for soft, flexible, and poised strength that does not equate punishment with completion of some difficult task. Your road might still be long and demanding, but, with *NextU*, it's also filled with more support, kindness, and even fun.

Breakthrough

What stumbling block or wall do you want to avoid?
Sometimes there is a barrier to face before change can occur. Maybe it's a pothole, maybe more like a wall. It doesn't matter whether it's a misguided assumption or a crushing life crisis. It prevents you from moving or even seeing any way forward. These are the times when you need to make a dramatic and important discovery.

Sometimes surmounting this barrier requires extra focus and energy; sometimes you have to dismantle it one block at a time; sometimes you have to discover a way around it; sometimes you have to learn how to befriend it.

NextU helps you play with some of these approaches so you can achieve a new perception of yourself and your situation. Imagine transporting your barrier to the moon, changing the physics of your reality. Now you can easily leap over it in a single bound. Breakthroughs are often needed in situations where you cannot see or believe there is any way out.

Again, it's important to remember that you've placed the barriers there because you needed them for some very important protective reasons. It's because of these reasons that you cannot have a breakthrough based on someone else's advice or because someone else tells you to. You need to see for yourself, scout out your own new territories, decide on your own routes, and have your own "Aha!" moment.

Popular culture is full of exhortations to break through limits, ignoring many of the personal costs involved. But when you discover alternative ways of responding for yourself, you'll have the important personal context that creates enough safety to break through the old laws governing your behavior. The *NextU* breakthrough exercises help you pop up to a whole new level, check out your new context, gather more data, refine your approach, then take some safe risks.

The net benefits

Find your own strength, clarity, and answers.
Whether you need inspiration, intervention, or a breakthrough, after you master the fundamentals, the benefits are the same. You'll feel calmer, be more confident in your capabilities, and feel better just being in your body. You'll be developing the muscles and courage involved in making different choices, widening the spectrum of what you believe is possible, and recovering your sense of play.

Self as iceberg

When I was in fifth grade, I remember the teacher conducting a lesson on the Titanic. She showed us a picture of an iceberg and explained that what you see is only ten percent of the whole. Most of it was not visible because it resided below the waterline. It was the other ninety percent that sank the Titanic.

The same metaphor can apply to how you see yourself. It's easy to focus on what's visible, but it's what's below the waterline of our perceptions that has a much greater impact on our lives. There are two ways this metaphor applies: the first is in regards to our biological systems, and the second applies to the ways our minds make meaning of the world.

Experiences that come from your biological senses and your nervous, circulatory, respiratory, musculature, and immune systems communicate powerfully, but not with words. Here are a few examples: Your immune system communicates with fevers or rashes. If you're in a near-accident, your adrenal system instantaneously prepares your body to react as if in an emergency, and you make decisions based on gut feelings. Like learning any foreign language, if you pay attention, listen deeply, and practice, you'll get feedback that helps you progress.

You have probably heard many times that we're only using a tiny fraction of our brain. But you probably haven't heard that one way to increase that percentage is by tuning in to other senses and systems or what you are feeling. The key is increased curiosity, which means holding an open mind, inquiring, and listening to yourself.

The catch is that there is no dictionary offering easy translations: You have to suspend the urge to predict the outcome and jump to conclusions so that you're able to grasp meaning from the experience. Your answers are going to come from different sources than you may be accustomed to. For example, you may notice a change in your breathing, tension level, or sense of calm. An emotion might arise; you might feel lighter or heavier; you might have a sense of being able to see more at the periphery or feel more aligned with what is authentic.

While this ambiguity may generate some anxiety, there is also huge freedom because there is no "right" answer. Any investigation will yield at least breadcrumbs marking your way to clarity. This book is specifically designed to help you develop your skills of investigating, clarifying, reflecting, integrating, and acting just a little differently.

The other way to apply the iceberg metaphor is with how the brain forms beliefs that drive behavior. The visible part of the iceberg is behavior. Below the waterline your thoughts, emotions, beliefs, assumptions, and data you deem significant determine your behavior and view of reality.

The following anecdote on how quarks were discovered exemplifies how our beliefs determine what we think is possible. Scientists used to believe that nothing was faster than the speed of light. Then a few started challenging this assumption. When they shifted their beliefs, suddenly the ways and means of finding something faster opened up, and, indeed, they found particles that exceed the former limit. This illustrates why it's important to use *NextU* to help you become familiar with the deeper layers of your beliefs—so that you can manifest something that you think impossible.

Summary

This chapter explores and focuses on why people want to change, namely to start, stop, or avoid something. It explains that what helps ignite a change and what helps keep it going are the three catalysts of change: intervention, inspiration, or breakthrough. In addition, it explains the challenge and promise of getting beneath the surface of the familiar, increasing our awareness around more of our biological systems, as well as understanding the deeper drivers of our behavior.

Chapter 3

Laying the Foundations

Defining important words and concepts

Pause. Settle. Open.

One of the greatest keys to understanding yourself or others is to define important words. Words are symbolic. Because you and others around you speak English, you expect others to understand the meaning of your words. But when you send someone to the grocery store to get milk, he or she might not return with the version of milk you expected.

This very simple example demonstrates how the meaning of the word "milk" varies by individual. For example, it might mean nonfat or whole or organic to you, and something different to someone else. If you're a parent who has instructed a child to clean his or her room and been dissatisfied with the results, you have seen how your child's definition of clean probably diverges from your own. The assumptions you make about exactly what you hold in common could lead to greater clarification of the situation or they could lead to conflict.

Throughout the exercise section, you are reminded to first pause, settle, and connect to yourself. Understanding the words "pause, settle, and open" is key to getting the most out of these exercises. In the *NextU* method, these words represent whole processes.

The purpose of this chapter is to explain those words and processes so that you can get the most out of doing them. The intention is to help you understand why these simple directions are significant and how they enhance your results.

Who this chapter is for

If you're familiar with meditation, guided imagery, or centering techniques, you know how rewarding it is to pause during your day, settle, and connect more deeply to yourself. These are also preparation steps for *NextU* exercises. If you're accustomed to these practices, either skip this section or continue reading and deepen your understanding.

If these concepts are new to you, this section unpacks these concepts with explanations about how and why to do them. The paragraph above indicates some of the benefits. If you start each exercise by putting the rest of your life on pause, settling into your seat, and listening to yourself more deeply, you will be giving yourself huge gifts: time just for you, space to just be as you are, and awareness of what is going on inside you.

How to become present

If you ever took ballet, yoga, or martial arts, or pursued a sport, you know there are basic positions and combinations of movement, breath, and awareness that build a foundation through regular practice. The foundation sought for *NextU* is presence. This section details a few of those techniques that will help you become more present by cuing your body and mind.

You can spend less than a minute doing each *NextU* exercise. However, each step is a powerful practice that could produce profound effects. The techniques are drawn from a wide variety of sources ranging from traditional Buddhist, Hindu, and Jewish meditation; Reichian, Transpersonal, and Gestalt psychology; child development and change theories; theater games; ballet and modern dance; and tai chi and yoga, to name a few.

The *NextU* exercises are also widely used in stress-reduction programs. While the exercises are undeniably "lite" in that they don't take very long to do, *NextU* is designed to provide a taste of what might be possible if you choose deeper study. *NextU* will help you sample the allure of more presence in your life.

As you explore this section, consider experimenting with the difference it makes for you to spend two or twenty minutes on this step. The goal of this phase of the exercise is to set up the right conditions so that you have a successful experience. Success in this context is having the ability to free yourself from your automatic response and to expand the ways you get to "know" something.

Scientists will tell you that controlling the environment of their experiment is at least as important as doing the experiment. It's a good idea to have a space where you will be safe, quiet, and uninterrupted.

The three foundational activities—pause, settle and open—send messages to your brain, nervous system, and musculature to calm, quiet, and release, thereby creating an internal space and increased sensitivity. This creates the conditions that enable you to notice something other than the swirl of your usual activity. In other words, you can be present to what is actually happening in your life.

The purpose of this section is to help you understand how to become present and why it makes a difference. Here is an overview:

Pause

- Stop doing everything else.
- Put your judgment and expectations on hold.

Settle

- Be here, in this moment, exactly as you are.

Open

- Become curious and suspend judgment.
- Explore the exercise.
- Notice what you experience.

PAUSE

Stop doing everything else

This means give yourself permission to have at least one full minute all to yourself. No multitasking. Turn off your phone. Quit your email. Put your to-do list on hold. It means take yourself and your life seriously for sixty seconds. One minute is about eight to ten cycles of your breath.

You may notice that even thinking about taking one full minute just for you has an effect. If the only thing you do as a result of reading this book is to stop for a minute before starting your car or looking at your mobile device and tell yourself, "This minute is just for me," and then savor ten cycles of your breath, you will have reduced stress enormously.

Lest you think of that as a waste of time, consider the following. You have probably waited for more than a minute while at a traffic light, holding for customer service, or waiting for a website to load. Why not give one minute of your time and focus to yourself?

Put your judgment and expectations on hold

Judgments, criticism, and expectations are ways that you make sure you "measure up" to an ideal, and they are ways that you dominate and control your mind. Suspending them is a powerful way to get into the present moment. Doing so enables you to learn the unexpected, and perhaps even find a solution to a problem that you were only half aware existed.

You may or may not be able to turn your thoughts off. That is not important. What is important is to experience how you can slow your thoughts down and/or create some space; when you catch your mind racing away again, you can intervene and bring your focus back to the exercises.

Here is an example of how to do it.

Remember a time when you thought something like:

- This is stupid.
- What a waste of time.
- This will never work.
- I should be doing something different.
- I already know this.

Instead of what you usually do with these kinds of judgments, thank your brain for being so effective at getting things done. Tell it you are giving all your critical thoughts a one-minute rest, and you'll pick them all up again when you finish. Notice whether that helps quiet the chatter and, then, how having a little more space or quiet feels.

Theater directors know that the key to getting an audience to go along with a plot is something called the willing suspension of disbelief. You need to do that, too. All your rational mind may be screaming, "This is stupid," but when you risk being stupid, you can get smarter, sooner.

Because you're looking for something other than your instinctual response, observe your experience with curiosity rather than interpretation. This means asking sincere open questions and listening deeply and non-judgmentally for the response. Now that you've created a little space, you can settle in for the exploration.

SETTLE

Become familiar with this moment and yourself.
Be here, in this particular moment, exactly how you are. Back in the '60s, Ram Dass famously wrote, "Be here now." Cognitively, this rarely happens; your left brain is on overdrive, racing backward to the past or leaping into the future. Right now is the only moment you can change or truly live.

If you accept this premise, its corollary is here and now are the time and place for the life you most want to have. Even if it is only an instant, now is the only place to add drops of satisfaction. That is why it's worth practicing more awareness and appreciation of the present. The first lesson is to quiet your powerful and critical thought habits and listen to yourself.

Assess your present moment. What dominates your thoughts right now? Are you:

- Trying to revise the past?
- Worrying about the future?
- Trying to change someone else's behavior?
- Obsessing about something you cannot change?

Similarly, assess the state of your body right now:

- Where are you sitting on the chair?
- What sensations are you aware of?
- How would you describe your breath?
- How easy or tense is your body?

What did you notice? Chances are your thoughts were running all over the place or, perhaps, stuck in a familiar hamster wheel-like cycle. You may have realized that you don't feel your body at all, or that you are barely breathing. At this point the important things are to acknowledge where you are right now and what happens with the suggestion of even a little change.

Now that you have assessed your general state, the next step encourages your brain and body to slow down.

How to settle

- Sit in a chair.
- Ground yourself.
- Breathe more.
- Reduce outside stimulation.

The practice of settling starts with instructions to sit in a chair, put your feet flat on the floor, and take a couple of breaths. When you do these things, you are literally and figuratively supporting yourself in very important ways. You stand on solid ground. Once you understand the directions and appreciate the effects, you can use the practice of anytime and anywhere to plug into more emotional, intellectual, and neurological support.

This stability helps you counter the fight or flight response and triggers a biological response that you are safe and can keep calm. Think of a crying baby and how the simple act of swaddling and holding it helps it calm down. Once calm, it quickly becomes happy or curious, or falls asleep.

Sit in a chair

Every electrician knows that they need to ground electrical equipment to the earth. Since your nervous system works chemically or electrically as well, grounding yourself also helps to discharge excess nervous energy, which will also increase your steadiness and clarity. One of the simplest and most effective ways to do this is to increase your conscious contact with the ground.

When you sit fully in a chair, it signals to your nervous system that you are changing gears and entering a safe place. Choose a chair proportionate to your body size. Your chair's back should support your back. If not, put a pillow in between, so you have contact. If the chair has arms, make sure they allow your shoulders to be at ease. If not, don't use them.

When you sit with clear intention, you can lower the alert, which allows you to settle into yourself. Here is direction in more detail:

- Put your feet flat on the floor or on a book or block.

- Imagine increasing contact with the floor, seat, and back of the chair.
- Notice the effects.

This is an introduction to a wealth of techniques you can use to feel more grounded—and a few more follow. They are incredibly powerful to use on their own in stressful situations, such as during meetings, while speaking in public, or when you're in conflict with a family member. They will help you get focused and feel ready to pay attention to someone or something else.

Two simple grounding exercises:

Remember being on a beach.

> *Remember the feeling of running your feet through the warm sand. Imagine nestling your feet into the sand and wiggling your toes in a pleasurable way. Notice the effects of this visualization.*

Ground your body's electricity. Imagine a current going through your body and down into the ground.

> *Imagine that the electrical flow is penetrating deeper and deeper into the ground. Imagine going through the topsoil into the crust, the mantle, and all the way to the core. Notice how you feel.*

Breathe a little more

Your breathing is your barometer of aliveness. If your breath is shallow, you probably won't feel very much. When you are angry or holding something back or sitting in a dentist's chair, you may notice you are hardly breathing at all. Conversely, the more freely, fully, and easily you breathe, the more aliveness is available. Think about how you feel after a brisk walk or good run

You don't have to go out on a 5K run to prepare for a *NextU* exercise. Just taking a few breaths, just a little deeper, just a little easier, with just a little more release, can awaken your awareness and increase your pleasure. A few very simple, highly portable ways to explore this ready resource follow.

Play with your breath:

Sigh.

> *Take a big breath in. Open your mouth. Drop your jaw. Sigh the air out in a gush. Repeat three times. As you come back to regular breathing, pause, and notice the effects.*

Gently expand your capacity.

> *Fill and empty your lungs, stretching your capacity just a little more each time. Then let your breathing come back to normal, noting how it feels to have more air move through your body.*

Breathe with your back.

> *For the next thirty seconds or so, just observe your breath. Notice that you mostly breathe from the front of your chest, in spite of the fact that your lungs are three dimensional. For the next four breaths, experiment and see if you can inhale into the back of your lungs. Try to make your back*

ribs expand. Then, allow your breath to return to normal and notice any effects.

Add more ease.

Carefully observe your breathing right now. Is it shallow or deep? What parts of your body are moving in response? Does it feel easy or labored? How else might you describe it? Now that you have taken note of where you are, imagine that with each breath you can add just a little more ease. Repeat this for the next eight breaths.

The most important guidance is to be gentle. Conscious breathing is a great warm-up exercise for change, as it literally makes space in your body for something new to happen. Your body is like a bathtub; if it's already full, adding more to it will only make it overflow. You have to let some water out first.

A few **NextU** exercises are explicitly breathing exercises. Allowing yourself to breathe more fully and freely is one of the most fundamental things you can do to improve all aspects of your thinking, feeling, and functioning body.

Deep breathing is the gateway to more feeling. While it's enlivening, it has other possible side effects. Fiddling with your breath can make you dizzy or it can bring up emotions.

You are always in control

Emotions are a natural indicator of aliveness. However, if you're not accustomed to feeling emotions, it might feel as if you're losing control. Remember, you are always in control. You can always stop the practice or do it with less intensity if you feel anxious. If you can tolerate the discomfort, you can work with it.

If you can, acknowledge any uncomfortable feelings and increase your compassion. Imagine yourself surfing on top of the feeling as if it were a wave until you reach the shore. Another alternative is to just give over to a good cry or go get your tennis racquet and whack a bed. If you consistently feel overwhelmed when doing these exercises, this might be a signal that you would benefit from some added professional help.

Reduce outside stimulation

It's innate to react to outside stimulation, so not reacting to what's going on around you is counter to your biological wiring. However, removing the burden of processing all that information gives you space to discover new alternatives. There are three easy ways to decrease the stimuli: close your eyes, reduce the volume, and put out the "do not disturb" notice.

Close your eyes.

Your brain is wired to focus more on external stimuli, so closing your eyes will help you keep your attention on the exercise Closing your eyes helps change your focus to what's happening internally and helps you to stay with your experience. If you don't like closing your eyes, you can reduce the external stimulation by lowering your eyelids until they are nearly closed.

Reduce the volume.

Your ears are a primary way that you identify threats. Find as quiet and safe a space as possible. Turn off electronic devices. The act of turning off the devices also is a signal to yourself that you can let go of the continual scanning for the external demands of the world, and it frees you to focus on the internal conversation.

> *Send a "do not disturb" message to yourself and others.*

Give yourself permission to have a small increment of time completely to yourself. Whether you feel an external or internal urge to interrupt, hold steady. If it's really important, it will still be there in a minute.

OPEN

Explore with the intention of finding something new
The verb explore invites you to be curious, go where you haven't been before, engage with the intention of learning something, and play. Play is essential to your success, because when you're really playing, you suspend judgment.

Success in changing yourself means you have to give up always thinking you are "right" about your thought or behavior. It's habitual to judge things in advance of trying them. You may already be thinking that this will never work, it's stupid, or that you already know it all. That may be correct. But if something more is calling you, then experiment and be deeply curious. If the process feels good, enjoy it for its own sake without jumping to future conclusions.

Playing is like dancing. If all you do is run around and move to music, you have fun. If you learn some of the steps, you add satisfaction. If you develop your technique, the whole experience expands and you'll have the knowledge to keep growing on your own.

This book is about the most familiar and simultaneously the least known thing in the world: yourself. Like scientific investigation, you don't really know which data points are going to be of most value, so you need to learn to pay attention to as much new information as possible.

Here are a few images to prepare you for your adventure. Imagine:

- Using the delicacy needed to explore a single snowflake
- Being the first human to land on Mars
- Seeing hidden potential in everything you touch
- Noticing the significance of each shift, tiny or large.

Notice what you experience

Noticing requires that you observe broadly and keenly. Be objective, as if you were viewing the experience like a movie camera, taking in actions but not assigning motives. What changed? Where are the changes? What are the results of those changes?

When you do the exercises with care for yourself and the intention to learn from them, you'll derive many benefits. Even if all you do is stop and breathe with focus and attention for a full minute you will radically change your life. Beyond the doing, noticing the effects will help you connect the dots about what works for you. Then, when you recognize a desirable effect, you'll know how to repeat or expand it.

Noticing involves creating meaning for yourself out of your observations. Remember, you are translating a language that only you can understand. It takes a lot of practice. It may feel silly or you may feel filled with uncertainty; it may be easier to belittle or ridicule yourself than to validate your genuine experience, whatever that is. Try to remain curious and experimental, rather than jump to some conclusion.

If you wonder what you're supposed to notice, here are a few suggestions:

- Level of and location of tension
- Ease or difficulty of breathing
- Speed or harshness of your thoughts
- Thoughts that come to mind
- Different sensations
- Memories or ideas sparked
- Level of comfort, calm, or optimism

If you feel frustrated by the speed of your progress, think of how many times a baby says, "buh, buh," or "ba, ba, ba" before it finally says something like "water." Researchers say that it takes at least ten thousand repetitions of something to find mastery. How many attempts do you allow yourself before you give up, saying you have no talent?

You are the greatest investigator of you, so take a few moments to reflect and collect. You might want to write a little or a lot. You might want to keep a journal, order the workbook companion from me, scribble on the back of an envelope, or share your experience with a buddy.

Scientists write down their observations because looking at individual data does not yield to patterns or hypotheses. It takes many experiments. The recent concerns about climate change came about as a result of many years of collecting details and looking at them over time.

Most importantly: *Start*

There's no better time than right now. There's no better way than the way you do it now. There's no more pressing need than whatever you feel right now.

Starting is not a cavalier act. It invites you to open your mind to the possibility of something different and to take action. Action is a risk, so starting is an act of courage, each and every time. Starting implies faith, however faint, in an ending that's at least a little better. Starting means opening the gate, preparing to dive, saying yes. It's the momentum of commitment.

This chapter may seem like a lot of overhead to pile onto exercises that only take a few minutes. However, greater understanding of your context will help you get the most out of your practices. From now on, simple reminders will do. You now have the short code that unlocks a big gate: *Pause. Settle. Open.*

Chapter 4

The NextU Exercises

Below you'll find a list of common limiting thoughts that alert you that something is out of balance. If you want to find an alternative to running down the same old rat hole, you can refer to the accompanying *NextU* exercise. You will find an explanation of the alternative and step by step instructions in how to transform your experience of yourself in the moment. You may want to read the whole chapter through from start to finish or you may want to find a limiting thought that you identify with and skip right to it, so you can address it right now.

Each of these exercises can be done in a minute, but you may find added benefit if you spend more than a minute on them. The point is, it doesn't take much time to get started with meaningful change!

The Limiting Thoughts

The Limiting Thought:

I don't have a passion

What thoughts come to mind when you hear the advice "listen to your vocation" or "follow your bliss"?

A common response is something like, "I'm just one of those people who don't have a passion" or "I don't have a calling." Today, that may be true; however, these beliefs shield you from the messages that your life generates.

These beliefs put your life's phone on mute; you're never aware of all the calls that are coming in all the time. The first step is to free yourself from the Hollywood version and welcome what authentically delights and excites you.

The way to find out about your passion is to increase your receptivity to the signals your life broadcasts all the time. There are billions of bits of data coming at you all the time. Pay attention to them: What attracts your attention? What evokes an emotional response? What rouses your curiosity?

Noticing what you notice is subtle and powerful, and it requires practice. But the more you acknowledge and notice these things, the clearer the signals become.

One-Minute Transformation:

Your life is talking to you all the time

Pause. Settle. Open.

Start where you are now. As much as you can, validate yourself and your experience. Each attempt will reveal more stepping stones.

Use your breath to soften your mind and body. Assume that you have many callings in life. Give yourself permission to have very ordinary or small things fill you with enthusiasm or delight.

Some answers may come clearly. Or, you may experience a rush of judging thoughts or hear nothing. In the first case, mentally, turn the volume down and reassure yourself that it is totally safe to name your passion. In the other, slow down the speed at which you are listening. Listen to what your life is telling you about your passions right now. Then mentally complete the following sentences:

I am always curious about...

I use my free time to...

The Limiting Thought:

I wouldn't be any good at that

One of the secret signs that you're getting closer to uncovering something important to you is when you hear yourself think or say, "Oh, I wouldn't be any good at that." For some reason, you believe that you must be a high achiever before you even start to try something.

Remember when you saw a child trying to throw a ball for the first time? He or she was probably not trying to fulfill a requirement to get it "right" or be "good enough." The child was just delighted to try again and again and again. You have that capability, too. However, something got in the way—perhaps a need to be perfect, to save face, or not be a loser.

While this strategy protects you from jeers from peers and siblings, it effectively stonewalls your inner desires. What if the whole point wasn't to be perfect, but to keep fooling around, experimenting, engaging, and having fun just because it delights you?

One-Minute Transformation:

Play more

Pause. Settle. Open.

Remember a time in your life when you had fun playing. As you inhale, imagine you're reinflating the memory of how you lived immersed in fun.

Imagine that clumsy attempts, near-misses, wild pitches, and off-track explorations are necessary and delightful stages of learning.

Through the next eight cycles of breath, imagine that with each exhale you're clearing out the judgments and barriers inside yourself that inhibit your ability to play. With each inhale enjoy the increased space inside yourself to be silly, to make bold statements, to step off the high dive and risk not looking good.

How has increasing the feeling of play affected you? Notice your breath, thoughts, face, and the rest of your body.

What is one very easy, small, simple way to be playful today?

The Limiting Thought:

Nothing will ever change

When life is tough, sometimes it feels like everything is falling apart. One mishap follows another—you lose all your data, your furnace fails, a sale falls through, you get a traffic ticket. This string of events leads you to believe that the deck is stacked against you. You conclude that things will never change and you're doomed.

These beliefs contradict the laws of nature. Change is inevitable and inexorable. Everything changes, although like continental drift or the climate, it can be hard to see it happening in the moment. You need to take a longer view and consider your whole life to appreciate the sometimes slow evolution of change.

Signs of progress aren't necessarily found in your place of pain or in the thing you identify as your problem. The real problem is that your imagination is stuck on right now, this one problem, or "It's not perfect," so you'll need to find ways to let in more information. For example: expand your time horizon, context, and appreciation of what is already emerging.

One-Minute Transformation:

It's already happening

Pause. Settle. Open.

Expand your time horizon. Unroll your life timeline five or ten or twenty years back to the time you first got the inkling you wanted a change. Imagine planting the desire as seeds and that you can see underground. Notice when those seeds germinated and sprouted. Perhaps, they required a season of dormancy before taking root.

Allow your mind to move forward along your life timeline. Take note of decisions, events, relationships, learning that nourish your seeds. Notice how they have matured over your time span and what might be impeding their growth.

As you attend to your seedlings what can you learn about might support even more success?

Specifically, how is your change unfolding today?

What do you want to encourage, and how will you do those things?

The Limiting Thought:

Nobody loves me

Sometimes you may feel lonely, left out, or like no matter how hard you try, you never get to be "the special one." You begin to believe that there's something genetic making you unlovable.

This conclusion is a gross misinterpretation of your biology. Your interdependent systems, including all of your cells, depend on you being exactly as you are and adore you for succeeding at being you. These living entities work tirelessly on your behalf—hanging on your every breath, attending to your every need.

In other words, you have a posse of some three to ten trillion adoring fans with you at all times. Their sole function is to support and encourage you in the most intimate ways. They are utterly devoted to you—just for being alive!

One-Minute Transformation:

Listen to your trillion rabid fans

Pause. Settle. Open.

Allow your breath to move effortlessly and be delicately pleasurable.

As you breathe, consider all the amazing and different systems at work in your body that are affected by your breathing—respiratory, circulatory, sensory, neurological, muscular, skeletal, and hormonal, to name a few.

Feel how well each system serves you and how finely tuned each is to your unique needs. Imagine you have a special device that allows you to see and hear individual cells.

Your cells have a special message for you. What are they saying to you?

How does it feel to have a trillion adoring fans?

The Limiting Thought:

I know that already

Do you have the "right-answer reflex?" When someone poses a problem, are you first to have the right answer? It worked well in math class, but it doesn't work so well when you want something other than the results you've been getting.

When you give in to the right-answer reflex, you get a litany of the usual responses just like always. The immediate right answer is a kind of trap: It limits you to the solutions and knowledge of the past.

It's been called insanity if you do the same thing over and over and expect different results. When looking for a different result, you need to find a way to inhibit the immediate "I know that already," right-answer response.

The first step is to create the mental space for something novel to enter your consciousness, which requires risking dissolving your certainty. It means you have to blur the edges of your ideas about how things are "supposed" to be and what you "should" do.

One-Minute Transformation:

Risk not knowing

Pause. Settle. Open.

Imagine that you can soften all of your boundaries. Give yourself permission to be in a state of not knowing.

Imagine you're receiving a faint message in an unknown language. Visualize the receiving capacities of your ears and increase their ability to tune in.

This message is just for you. Allow in whatever information comes to you, whether it's an image, sensation, sound, texture, movement, or words. Pause.

Try not to assign meaning or value to this message right away. Just receive and record it. Maybe the meaning is obvious. Perhaps it's opaque or incomplete.

What inklings did you receive?

What unusual information came to mind?

What's your message?

The Limiting Thought:

Smile!

Think of all the times someone has pointed a camera at you and ordered, "Smile!" You probably didn't always feel like smiling, but did so regardless.

The ability to put on a face that is out of alignment with what is going on inside you may help you fit in socially. However, wearing a mask also has a cost. The mask is rigid and impermeable, which means you limit expression and connection.

Perhaps you have experienced going to a party with your mask on, interacting with other people, yet feeling lonelier than ever when you come home.

The mask prevents you and others from knowing and cherishing the authentic you beneath it.

You have to take the mask off in order to nourish your inner self. Besides, softening into who you really are under the surface leads to a much more genuine and inviting smile.

One-Minute Transformation:

Take off the mask

Pause. Settle. Open.

Imagine that there is a fountain of energy flowing up your spine and neck balancing your head like a ball at the top. As you breathe, allow your head to delicately move back and forth on the spray. Notice the sensation of lightness and support.

As your head feels more support, allow the tension in your neck and face to ease and release.

Soften your tongue and imagine it relaxing all the way down into your throat. Allow your jaw to release. Visualize more room for your teeth in your mouth.

Imagine your skin softening and expanding.

Soften even more.

Now, sense the face beneath the face you present to the world.

What do you notice?

The Limiting Thought:

Don't bother trying

Some people learned early in life that failing was a sure route to ridicule or exclusion. Perhaps you couldn't throw a ball well or run fast or draw a realistic-looking horse. Trying meant risking being picked last for the team, being told not to sing out loud, or being belittled in some other way. So you stopped trying, which made it really hard to consider, let alone follow, a dream of something impossible.

The best way to see dreaming in action is to watch babies. Babies continually reach out with optimism. Optimism is the belief that the world wants to celebrate us as we are, rather than how we're "supposed" to be.

As babies move from babbling to talking, they're not waiting to speak comprehensible words. They keep gathering skills and practicing with pride about wherever they are again and again and again.

Instead of telling yourself, "It will never happen for me, so why even try?" you can keep experiencing the joy of optimistic learning and imagining the world responding, "That was great. Keep going!"

One-Minute Transformation:

Reach out with optimism

Pause. Settle. Open.

Think of something you would secretly love to do. Visualize a specific person, real or imagined, who totally adores and supports you.

Now imagine having a conversation with that person about that secret.

- ▶ Imagine that person responding, "Yes. Of course you should do that. Bring me with you every step of the way. "

- ▶ Look around at your environment and imagine that everyone and everything is saying, "Yes, of course. You should do that. Reach out a little."

- ▶ Imagine releasing any contradictory "but" like a soap bubble. Trust that you have unconditional support for tens of thousands of learning attempts.

What do you notice when you reach out with this kind of optimism?

The Limiting Thought:

Nothing is working

There are days when it seems like nothing goes your way. Perhaps you even feel like you've taken several steps backwards. At those times, it's easy to believe you lack some basic connections, skills, or genes to make life flow successfully.

Within the belief that nothing is working is a gift hidden in plain sight: it's your "nothing." Instead of resisting and being angry about everything you perceive you don't have, you can get curious. Nothing is a very interesting place when explored for its own unique qualities.

Instead of a dead end, it's a blank slate. You can stop burdening yourself with expectations of how it's supposed to be. Instead of a sentence of doom, it's an invitation to play.

What might happen in a space of pure potential?

When you thoroughly explore the concept of nothing, you may notice the tension in your face has softened, and the vise grips on your brain have already loosened, making space for "something."

One-Minute Transformation:

Explore the nothing

Pause. Settle. Open.

Follow your breath for a couple cycles of inhalations and exhalations, noticing how fully or shallowly you're breathing. Continue this conscious breathing throughout the exercise.

Imagine that you have received a beautifully wrapped package. Give yourself a moment to appreciate how wonderful it is.

Now open it. There is nothing inside.

Instead of throwing it aside, explore the "nothing." Allow its qualities of shape, color, texture, temperature, and/or sound to become apparent.

Consider that *nothing* is actually an extremely valuable gift just for you. Give yourself permission to get inside and explore it.

What benefits have you already received from this gift?

What unique opportunities does it suggest?

What do you notice about your nothing?

The Limiting Thought:

I need to escape

Remember that great vacation or weekend away? What was it that you valued so much about the experience?

Perhaps it was the time, rest, quiet, and deep connections. Perhaps it was the new sights, sounds, smells, and how you experienced yourself. Or perhaps it was something totally different.

While long vacations are extremely valuable to mental and physical health, they are not always possible when you need a break. What if you could take a tiny concentrated dose of your great experience any time you want an escape?

The active ingredient in this remedy is your sense of wonder. Wonder occurs when you see something anew. It is visceral. Awe silences the mental chatter. You see and sense more. The feeling is pleasurable and renewing.

If this sounds attractive, you don't need to plan a getaway sometime in the future. You can have it now, in one minute.

One-Minute Transformation:

Create a wonder break

Pause. Settle. Open.

You can take a wonder break anytime with a little preparation:

- ► Soften everything to make more room for the unexpected.
- ► Pretend that you do not already know every answer.
- ► If your mind wanders, gently bring it back to the exercise.

Allow something in your field of vision to interest you. Instead of seeking it out, allow it to come to you. During your next five breaths, get very curious by noticing details that you have never considered before, for example:

- ► Notice how your selection carves out or affects the space around it.
- ► Sense this object with your tongue or heart or elbow.
- ► Allow your eyes and face to soften even more, so that you can perceive the specific qualities of your object more vividly and deeply.

What do you notice now that you would like to continue in the future?

The Limiting Thought:

Do

I just have to _____. What verb do you fill in the blank with? Is it related to the list of things you believe you must complete?

The dirty secret is that "doing" just leads to the need to do more. Lists have a habit of being self-generating and somewhat insatiable. There is an alternative to checklist living: You can "be" in your life, imperfect and unfinished as it is.

Being in your life is not empty in terms of worth, rather, it creates space to allow yourself to connect to and appreciate your aliveness. For example, you get to absorb the richness of your current experience instead of rushing to the next thing and/or turn off the mental emergency monitoring system that continually scans your horizon trying to control what might be next.

You cannot check off an authentic life as if it were a to-do list. But you can start experiencing it, one moment at a time.

One-Minute Transformation:

Be

Pause. Settle. Open.

One way to practice *being* is to relax. You will get to a deeper level of relaxation if you can lie down, but you can relax in any position.

To start, close your eyes. Imagine becoming heavier and heavier with each exhalation. Allow yourself to give in to the heaviness. Release and relax a little more with each breath. Without any effort, allow the air to fill your lungs just as your body wants.

Take eight breaths in this state, which should last about one minute. Allow the sensations and insights of being at rest to fill you.

Very slowly and gently, open your eyes. If you are lying down, roll onto your side for a moment before you get up.

What changes or insights did you notice from relaxing for at least a full minute?

Try doing this for three, five, or ten minutes or longer.

The Limiting Thought:

I'm stuck

In a culture that values progress and getting ahead, feeling stuck is not discussed in polite company. Besides, if you mention feeling stuck, it usually elicits lots of great ideas that other people believe would help you find your way back to the racetrack. However, these ideas, regardless of how good they are, are not what you really need. What you most often need is a way to break up the mental logjam that impedes your flow.

What holds the jam in place are shame and frustration. Most likely, the jam has occurred because you are somewhere completely new. In fact, the jam could be thought of as a milestone, not a sinkhole.

Your wall of shame dissolves in the presence of self-acceptance. It reveals chinks, trickles, and gaps in your defenses where water naturally finds a way through. The more you explore the places where your flow is, no matter how minuscule, the more alternatives, dynamics, and strategies you uncover.

One-Minute Transformation:

Find the flow

Pause. Settle. Open.

Envision what is keeping you stuck, without needing to change or judge it. How big is it? How solid? How familiar or new? What does it feel like in relation to you?

Imagine opening the faucet of your compassion; it doesn't matter whether it is full blast or a tiny drip. Follow it's flow as it meets your barrier. Watch how it gets through—or around—your blockage.

Mentally follow the seeps, drips, or trickles to where they join up with the main stream again. Congratulate yourself on your ingenuity.

Look for other avenues. Notice places where space is expanding or shifting. Notice detours and other ways the water is able to get around or break up your barrier.

What benefits does this nonlinear route offer you?

What new appreciation do you have for how you can move forward?

The Limiting Thought:

This is not the life I'm supposed to have

How does your life compare to the life you're supposed to have? You know, the happily-ever-after sort of life that is in the movies?

Real life might present a stark contrast to the movies. You may be faced with disappointment, difficulty, tragedy, and misfortune. You have "proof" that life is not fair. Perhaps you armor yourself against ever allowing that dissatisfaction to show. Still, however it's showing up right now; this is your life.

If you reject pain and suffering, you may think you're protecting yourself. However, you are actually preventing yourself from fully inhabiting the life you have. Real life includes disappointments, illness, losses, and struggles. Paradoxically, the more you accept and celebrate the whole of your life, warts and all, the more satisfying is your day-to-day experience.

Besides, this is the only life you have.

One-Minute Transformation:

Embrace the life you actually have

Pause. Settle. Open.

What part of your life do you wish you could surgically remove or reliably guard against?

Imagine that instead of needing to fight against it, this limitation is your greatest gift to you. In this vision, it holds the seeds of your freedom and fulfillment. You're supposed to live with it, learn from it, and allow it to help you grow.

Listen softly and deeply to the lesson it offers.

Instead of trying to hide it, imagine that your condition is like warm, luxurious sunshine that encourages you to expand. Appreciate all the new skills, wisdom, and direction it has propelled you into and how that makes you unique.

What differences do you notice?

What might be possible with your life as it is?

The Limiting Thought:

I always _____

There are many opportunities for you to disapprove of yourself—for example, breaking a dish, losing your keys, staining new clothes, or missing a deadline. One common response is to berate yourself with some version of, "I always do that!"

This reaction stems from a belief that you can punish yourself into perfection. However, this punishing-yourself-to-be-perfect strategy fails every time. In fact, the statement only reinforces that you will do it again.

There is another way: Impersonate the success you seek. Instead of being the vindictive disciplinarian starring in an unsupportive role, cast yourself as the benevolent fairy godmother.

Then, inhabiting that role, you can see what you might be currently blind to. When you experience holistic success, you can see the gaps between your old habits and what might be possible.

If I were a person who didn't lose her keys, what would I do with them first and foremost? What else would I be doing?

One-Minute Transformation:

Play the part of success

Pause. Settle. Open.

Think about one of your favorite ways of berating yourself.

Notice what you think and how you feel in your body when you berate yourself.

Now, imagine you have become the person who has the successful qualities or behaviors that you desire. Allow yourself to completely embody this character. How does that person breathe, think, and act?

Imagine interviewing the self you aspire to be. What does it take to be graceful, sensitive, thoughtful, or any other quality you desire?

What are the special skills that the successful you employs to make accomplishment automatic?

What do you notice about embodying your desired qualities?

How did you become that way?

The Limiting Thought:

I have no idea what I really want

As long as you're so tuned into what other people are saying you should aspire to, you can't hear the small, tender voice speaking about your own life.

The good news is that although that voice may be faint, your life persistently broadcasts information to you like a low-wattage radio station. You just may need different antennas, receivers and amplifiers to capture unfamiliar signals.

Tuning in to your frequency is risky. Your desires might be scorned as not "practical" or "cool." Your longings are tender little beings, and you'll need to have the courage to give them the appreciative nurturing they need.

Validate the small inklings that you feel. Play with them just like the game "Hot or cold?" Notice what draws your attention and how it gets "hotter." Let go of things when you have to work hard to heat them up.

One-Minute Transformation:

Tune in to your station

Pause. Settle. Open.

If you have no idea what you really want, perhaps it's because you're listening to the wrong channel.

Imagine that each inhalation allows you to release your muscles, eyes, ears, and tongue so you can increase your sensitivity and receptivity to a wider spectrum.

Imagine hearing a message in a different language on a different frequency. Perhaps this message is a sensation, rhythm, or pattern. Let yourself receive without deciding what it means.

Make a note of it. You're developing a new voice to comprehend many new experiences. The important thing is to receive whatever comes your way—and to thank yourself for listening.

What do you notice with your new voice and way of listening?

What makes it get "hotter"?

The Limiting Thought:

I'm a lazy-good-for-nothing

In one of my favorite children's books, Eleanor Estes' *The Little Oven*, Helene's mother would notice when she was tired or cranky and say, "I think it is time for a little 'ovin." Then she would gather Helene up in her arms and hold her. However, when Helene's friend asks her own mother for "a little 'ovin'," she gets a toy stove.

I misinterpret messages too. I'm still afraid of calling strangers on the phone, taking on big projects, and asking for what I really want. Instead of noticing the fear or feelings of being overwhelmed or disappointed, I try to punish myself into good behavior. You may be familiar with this habitual response.

What we all really need is a little 'ovin, in the words of Helene's mother. We need to physically or metaphorically gather ourselves up into a big hug. The hug communicates unconditional approval and safety. From this reassurance, you can expand beyond your fears, ask for what you need or want, or even cry a little.

One-Minute Transformation:

Time for a little 'ovin

Pause. Settle. Open.

Think of a behavior you judge as negative or nonproductive and how you usually react when it shows up.

Now, shift to a different possibility. Imagine that the behavior is just like an expression of a baby who needs to be held and comforted.

Imagine taking the baby into your arms and saying, "There, there. It will be all right." If you would like to increase the effects of this practice, physically cradle yourself and rock.

Now lavish yourself with compassion, patience, and comfort. Take four or five breaths, allowing more and more of those qualities to soak in.

What effects do you notice?

The Limiting Thought:

My life is in chaos

Sometimes it feels like a hurricane is on the shore of your life. It's difficult and terrifying to get through, and it leaves devastation in its wake. What you call "your life" is torn apart. You lose many anchors, clarity, relationships, and time for yourself.

When you're in an emergency, there is an overwhelming amount of challenges and feelings to attend to. Usually, you're powerless to do anything about changing the external circumstances. However, you retain the most important coping tool: your breath.

A few conscious breaths can change your experience and bring you into the present moment. Full and free breathing calms the nervous system, brings more oxygen into the lungs, and dispels carbon dioxide. Breathing more creates nanoseconds or minutes of calm and safety.

The beauty of this is that you can take a breath anytime, anyplace.

One-Minute Transformation:

One breath

Pause. Settle. Open.

Set your foundation with greater focus and intention than usual. Refer to Chapter 3 if you need suggestions on how to do this. Your body needs strong signaling that, at least in this moment, you are safe.

Regard yourself tenderly.

Very gently, allow a little more air in.

- ► Breathe so the air delivers comfort, safety and compassion.
- ► Continue for at least eight breath cycles.
- ► Now, allow your breath to return to normal.

Notice how you feel. Breathing more can calm you or bring up a desire to cry. If you can, allow the sadness to flow. If that seems too overwhelming, try to hold yourself very gently as if you were a baby.

How did you feel physically at the beginning?

What do you notice after a minute of breathing?

The Limiting Thought:

If only...

If only I were ten pounds lighter, if only I had an intimate relationship, if only I had lots of money, if only I could travel... then I would be happy.

It's common to believe that some specific thing is standing between you and true happiness. Perhaps you have postponed pursuing the happiness you want until you meet your standard.

The challenge is that even when you lose those pesky ten pounds or finally enter into a relationship, the unhappy parts of you don't disappear. You'll have the same ability to be happy then as you do today.

Happy people have a secret: They can find satisfaction now. They don't put off enjoying life because of current circumstances. When you stop limiting yourself because of a condition, you might start noticing that there are many people who do not see the same condition as a barrier to the experience you envy.

One-Minute Transformation:

Start now

Pause. Settle. Open.

Reflect for a moment on the past twenty-four hours.

Think of a moment that you would rate somewhere between *pleased* and *ecstatic* along the spectrum of happiness. It can be tiny or huge.

If you're having trouble, you might think about a sunset, a meal, a glass of wine, a conversation, a memory, or a sensation that made you feel good. Pick a specific incident.

Mentally replay the experience. Take four breaths, each one becoming deeper and slower. As you breathe, imagine getting more and more of the aspects of that experience that really make you happy.

Notice how it feels to have more happiness right now.

Try amplifying other experiences of happiness. Repeat, as needed, every day.

What do you notice?

The Limiting Thought:

I'm not worth it

One of your greatest acts of courage is to believe you're entitled to take the next step regardless of whether you feel you deserve it.

What do you have to prove to be worthy? You might notice that the bar is so high, it would require superhuman effort to reach it. While athletes may turn to drugs to achieve record-breaking results, you can enhance your performance with unconditional love.

Imagine your great-great-grandmothers. Think back to all they sacrificed and toiled for in hopes that their children and their children might thrive. You are the manifestation of their dreams. They are thrilled that you are alive today.

Allow yourself to receive their pride in your attempts, interest in each decision you make, and fierce encouragement to continue. Notice how the force of that unconditional love reduces the question of worthiness to dust.

Dose with unconditional love

Pause. Settle. Open.

Allow yourself to take a few gentle, nourishing breaths. Just for the span of this exercise, put your judgment on hold.

Call on a real or imagined ally, such as an unconditionally loving grandmother, to help. Imagine she is beholding you with complete attention and adoration.

Imagine whispering your fear of taking the next step to her. Hear her respond with delight, "Of course! Of course you can do that!" or "Go ahead. Fail often and early, so you can succeed sooner."

Notice the effects.

What is it like to have unconditional support?

What are you drawn to do next?

What might it be like to have an ally by your side through the next phase?

The Limiting Thought:

Get going already!

Great architects know that the entryway has a big impact on how comfortable people feel in a building. Likewise, you need a transition from outside to inside, or, mentally, from one task to another.

Generally, people are so busy rushing from the last thing to the next thing that they don't take the time to arrive. They launch into getting a meeting over with, for example, so they can rush to the next one.

The irony is that almost every meeting starts with "Welcome." What might happen if you arrived well?

One of the unintended consequences of not taking a moment for transition is that you actually spin your wheels instead of moving forward. You spend the first part of the meeting mentally reliving—and rewriting—the situation you just left or planning for the "more important" meeting you're headed to next.

When you take a moment to transition yourself into a new interaction, you're more relaxed, focused, and able to contribute in a meaningful way.

One-Minute Transformation:

Arrive Completely

Pause. Settle. Open.

In the privacy of your own mind, you can set some boundaries that will help you arrive and be ready. First, take charge of your time, deliberately end the activity before, and give yourself a moment to arrive in the new space or situation.

Here are a few experiments to try:

- ▶ Notice what holds your attention from new work.
- ▶ Schedule time to get from place to place.
- ▶ Arrive a minute early to your next meeting.
- ▶ Take a deep breath and sigh it out.

Notice the physical, mental, and emotional effects of creating time and space to arrive and be welcome.

What are the effects of giving yourself transition time?

What are the effects of consciously ending the previous activity or noting what needs to be done to resolve it?

The Limiting Thought:

How could she/he do that to me?

When someone does not respond to you the way you think a friend or lover should, you get righteously offended or "deeply hurt."

You mistakenly believe that the amount of time you spend thinking about yourself equals the amount of time other people spend thinking about you.

Actually, the opposite is true: People are so self-absorbed that they hardly notice anything beyond themselves and their own needs. While this may seem cynical, the good news is that by changing your assumptions about their motives, you can change your experience of the relationship.

When you assume good intentions, you free yourself from an hour or days of the "How could they do that to me?" song. Instead, you set up the conditions to be able to receive the gifts your loved ones are trying so hard to give you, communicate what you really want, and create experiences that have shared meaning.

One-Minute Transformation:

Assume the best intentions

Pause. Settle. Open.

Think about the last person who slighted you or a situation in which you didn't feel appreciated.

Feel how your body responds. Perhaps your jaw clenches, your breath gets shallower, your lips, neck, or diaphragm get tight. Perhaps you cannot think of anything else besides how "right" you are.

Now, imagine the person had good intentions for their behavior. Dare to imagine that their intentions were even better. Notice the effects on your breath, body, and mind. Experience any pleasure that may result.

What do you notice about changes in your body, mind, and emotions when you assume others have the best of intentions?

The Limiting Thought:

I don't have time

How often do you hear yourself say, "I don't have time for self-care"? Instead of the break you know you need, you eat vending machine food, take aspirin, or buy a latte. You postpone your needs—even though it would only take a minute.

You may be in a situation that demands that you postpone your comfort, like caring for a baby, working on an important project, juggling work, family, and school or some other passion. The tendency is to exclude yourself from the equation of all that needs to get done.

In the same time it takes to find and unwrap a piece of chocolate hidden in your purse or freezer, you can give yourself a micro-break. The micro-break comes with instant stress relief, a new perspective—and a positive effect on your waistline.

One-Minute Transformation:

Renew with a micro-break

Pause. Settle. Open.

Notice your breathing cycle.

Is it easy, shallow, jagged, held, or something else?

Remember a wonderful scent.

- ► Allow it to become vivid and to suffuse your body.
- ► Notice other sensations that accompany that memory.
- ► Soak in the pleasure of the experience.

When you are ready, come back to your current space.

Notice how you feel after just a few inspired breaths.

The Limiting Thought:

I did it again. I'm a complete failure.

"I got fired/laid off... I did it again... I cannot get it right... I'm a complete failure..."

Have thoughts like these ever been your personal soundtrack?

Notice in what ways you gave the person who judged you the power to determine your entire worth and the worth of any contribution you made or might make in the future.

Mentally, you cut off all the parts of you that are "bad," without realizing that the side effects are letting your sense of worth, safety, and possibility bleed out of you as well.

Call for emergency rescue.

Stop the bleeding with direct and continual application of compassion. Compassion blocks shame and other negative interpretations of events. Deep and overflowing kindness reintegrates all the parts of you, exactly as they are, including all of the imperfect and clumsy parts. You'll recognize that you're a being in progress.

One-Minute Transformation:

Triage with kindness

Pause. Settle. Open.

First-aid manuals all say to wrap a wound, apply pressure, and don't let up until the bleeding stops. Imagine that your own personal rescue team has arrived. Imagine them wrapping you in the gauze of compassion and holding you tenderly where you're hurting.

Feel yourself cocooned in cozy compassion, and soak it in. Every time a thought that shames or demeans you starts dominating your mind, take a breath and imagine soaking up more compassion from your dressings.

Turn it up more.

Turn it up even more.

Allow the compassion to suffuse you inside and out.

What do you notice when you hold yourself with compassion?

The Limiting Thought:

Be more productive

Our culture is obsessed with doing more. So you "push through" or you "give one-hundred and ten percent." The irony is that the route to more is by doing less.

It may seem counterintuitive, but relaxing is the key to concentrated, clear, constructive thinking. Physiologically, relaxation increases the amount of oxygen available to the body, increases the secretion of serotonin, the hormone associated with feelings of happiness, and it reduces stress. Relaxation enables you to direct your energy and free your mind from its rut.

Letting go is often a huge physical and emotional relief. At first, you'll feel the physical release of tension in your muscles. You may fall asleep or cry.

Then, you'll feel clearer and more energized. You might be able to see new options and be able to discern where your efforts are most important.

One-Minute Transformation:

Less is more

Pause. Settle. Open.

Let yourself intentionally relax for a minute.

While you'll reach a deeper level of relaxation if you can lie down, you can relax in any position. In a chair, adjust your body so that your feet are flat on the floor and your back is supported. Close your eyes.

Imagine that you're becoming heavier with each exhalation. Allow yourself to give in to the heaviness, so you release and relax a little more with each breath. Without any effort, allow the air to fill your lungs, as your body wants.

Repeat this cycle of getting heavier with each breath seven or eight times.

Before moving, notice any changes in how your body feels and the quality of your thoughts. Very gently, come back to whatever room you're in and resume your tasks.

What effects do you notice?

The Limiting Thought:

Stupid... bad... wrong... (repeat)

Who needs a judge, jury, or jail time when you condemn yourself? If the least shred of a real or imagined shortcoming or mistake sets off a tirade in your head of how worthless and unredeemable you are, then you are a candidate for an anti-bullying intervention.

In the words of June Ekman, you have to stop inviting the bully to your personal space. Instead, yell back: "Stop that! Stop bullying yourself! Yell back, punch the air—just inhibit that thought!"

You'll discover that when you yell back, you'll break through the force of your inner oppressor. You stop the tirade. You'll regain power and choice.

And, if no one is within earshot, you might assert yourself more strongly. Yell, "Stop it!" Use your arms to show you mean it. Stomp around the room.

One-Minute Transformation:

Become your bouncer

Pause. Settle. Open.

Don't let your mean self get away with bullying your tender, innocent, learning self. If you find you're thinking mean, self-limiting thoughts, intervene. You can be the bouncer at the door of your club.

Imagine yelling, "Stop it!" Notice the effects of thinking this statement.

To increase the effect, say it out loud. "Stop it!"

Practice inhibiting your usual pattern for one whole minute. If you hear the voice of the inner oppressor, yell again.

What do you notice when you think **"Stop it"**?

What do you notice when you say **"Stop it"** *out loud?*

What does intervening in this way free up?

The Limiting Thought:

Not now

How often do you say "not now" to your child, dog, or yourself?

The implicit message is that something else is more important. You become used to suppressing your needs and wants. Perhaps you can identify with some of these symptoms: You eat junk food instead of real meals. You run yourself into the ground instead of getting enough sleep. You drive yourself to do more instead of giving yourself time to exercise or spend time with the family.

Responding in a timely way to what your organism wants at a physiological level is at the foundation of health and well-being. It just requires you to make yourself as valuable as whatever else is going on.

When you do listen to that screaming inner child, you'll be surprised how quickly she calms down and how much better your task at hand goes. Just remember to occasionally listen when it's "me o'clock."

One-Minute Transformation:

It's "me o'clock"

Pause. Settle. Open.

Close your eyes for a moment and imagine all the important things you have to do, as if they were actual objects or boxes stacked up in front of you. Now, imagine that you are Photoshopping yourself into the picture.

Notice how big you are in relation to your tasks. Now, pick one specific task. Imagine making yourself much bigger in relation to it. Now make yourself much smaller. Pause to notice what changes as you change the scale.

Find a relationship that increases your comfort, humor, or confidence.

What happens when you are at least as important as your task?

What might you do when it is "me o'clock?"

The Limiting Thought:

It could be better

If one of your hobbies is to critique all the plays, movies, books, and/or meals you experience, you might be infected with the constant critiquing virus. Critical thinking is useful, and it can also be quite insidious. If it is leaking into the rest of your life, you might look for symptoms by reflecting on questions like these:

- ► How might my unreachable standards chip away at my relationships?
- ► How might my constant dissatisfaction prevent me from setting roots in my communities?
- ► How might I be robbing myself of just having fun?

Just like vaccinating yourself against the flu, you need to build a healthy immune response to perfection. Instead of examining what is wrong, change your focus to what is right. In other words, start appreciating things exactly as they are.

Each time you catch yourself critiquing, intervene with appreciation and more appreciation. Amazingly, the world will seem to get much better than it ever was when viewed through your critical thoughts.

One-Minute Transformation:

An appreciation vaccination

Pause. Settle. Open.

Appreciate some basics:

- ► Get quiet enough to sense your pulse.
- ► Consider the amazing job your heart does every moment.
- ► Sense the thousands of miles of circulatory system your blood pumps through every minute.
- ► Think of the number of cuts, scrapes, and burns your body has healed over your lifetime.

Bring your attention to something else in your immediate surroundings. Allow yourself to appreciate all the qualities it possesses and what it gives you. Let the appreciation sink in deeply.

If you really want an advanced practice, try appreciating the next red light you encounter.

Notice the effects of appreciating a few basic things.

What changes do you notice?

The Limiting Thought:

I'm in a satisfaction slump

Sometimes my experience of life is like a garden hose. If there's a kink in it, I feel cut off from the flow, depleted, and unappreciated. One way to untangle or unclog it is to give someone a gift.

All my life, spiritual and community leaders and—most frequently—my mother have told me to give more. Now, neuroscientists agree. Here is a highly simplified version of why. Low mood and low serotonin go together, so one way to get out of a slump is to increase your serotonin. When you give, it signals to the brain to release the neurotransmitter serotonin increasing your experience of pleasure and well-being.

The great thing is that giving does not stop with the production of a pleasant sensation. It also gives you a story that can make you feel good in an additional way. The real secret is that giving works even when you just imagine giving something.

One-Minute Transformation:

Pump up your pleasure—give more

Pause. Settle. Open.

Imagine giving someone a gift for no reason. Think of a specific person, perhaps someone you care about, a neighbor, or even some nameless person you encountered recently. Imagine wrapping a box with beautiful paper and a ribbon, placing the gift in their hands, and receiving their surprise and delight. Or imagine giving it surreptitiously and watching them discover it.

Notice the changes in your mood, energy, and attitude.

If you want to expand the practice, try giving someone an actual gift as small as a thought or expansive as a bouquet of flowers. Notice the effects on you at all stages of imagining, planning, giving, and receiving.

How does simply imagining giving affect you?

How does planning to give an actual gift affect you?

The Limiting Thought:

I blew my chance

If you examine the way you started a big learning project, perhaps you can identify with this process: "I'm willing to try—once. If I don't achieve the success I want and expect, I'll give myself a failing grade and give up."

New selfdom requires as much development and repetition as learning to play the guitar or competing in professional sports. It's not enough to get an insight; you have to learn how to absorb it into many cognitive, somatic, neurological, and other systems. It requires practice.

Practice means doing something over and over again until you figure out how to learn from experience. Practice means staying in the game when you're apparently not doing it right. Recognizing that you are not doing it right—yet—is, in fact, the gift of knowing what you need to work on now. Practice means continuing without judgment.

One-Minute Transformation:

Practice, practice, practice

Pause. Settle. Open.

Think of something that you secretly would love to do. Watch the procession of your thoughts in response to that dream.

Notice how you label yourself in relation to the activity or experience. Instead of focusing on those judgments, change your focus. What would you have to do if you were to start doing it?

What if the negative labels were absolutely necessary to your learning curve? How might it be praiseworthy to be clumsy, untalented, inept, thick, stupid, frustrated, slow, and/or a loser?

What does this approach encourage you to start?

How might you practice and reward yourself?

The Limiting Thought:

I'm stuck in my worst fears

Sometimes things don't feel like they're going to be okay; you feel crushed by circumstances. The only apparent choice is to let the situation squash you or run as fast as you can. These strategies lead to trapping yourself in your worst fears. One secret to getting out is to be curious.

Curiosity is the WD-40 for easing unmovable objects and thoughts. Your mind is programmed to respond with "fight or flight," but responding to challenges in life today requires more options. You start finding "more" by noticing and reversing your automatic assumptions: "I know…" or "I must control…" or "This is the way it is…"

Even by consciously thinking, "I wonder…" or "I'm curious…" you'll feel a physical change in your brain: It relaxes and opens. Curiosity cuts off the death spiral of your assumptions and slows your racing thoughts. When you follow your curiosity, "I wonder…" becomes a state of wonder, which leads to wonderful and takes you a long way from disaster.

One-Minute Transformation:

Liberally apply curiosity

Pause. Settle. Open.

Consider a challenge you have in your life.

Now imagine you're a being from a planet with an entirely different set of physical laws, such as gravity, number or placement of eyes, or life span, who has just landed on Earth.

Allow yourself to become curious about your challenge from this frame. Examine it as someone who has no knowledge of its symbolism or consequences and is trying to learn as much as you can about your new environment:

- ► What are its boundaries?
- ► How would it be useful?
- ► What does it respond to?
- ► Where does it lead?
- ► What can you learn from it?

What else are you curious about in terms of your challenge?

How might the alien resolve your challenge?

The Limiting Thought:

More. Do more.

Some people have a phobia about germs. Some fear being ordinary. The very thought raises alarms. Ordinary, they believe, means invisible and not doing enough to deserve love. If you identify, you also may notice that you always drive yourself to go a little beyond your expectations.

Striving turns out to be double-edged. On the one hand it means putting a great deal of energy into something, which generally has cultural value. On the other hand, striving is about struggle with no end. When you push yourself to get ahead, you also negate that you are sufficient.

Take a radical action: Dare to be ordinary.

When you let yourself be as you truly are, also known as your average, ordinary self, tension falls away. Striving often prevents you from being able to receive the love that you have been running after. You might even find there is time to fool around and have fun more.

Dare to be mediocre

Pause. Settle. Open.

Stop striving. Just for one minute, allow yourself to completely accept an invitation to be in the middle of your ordinary self.

For the next four cycles of your breath, imagine letting your breath nurture your core.

Over the next four cycles of your breath, release:

- ► Your head from getting ahead
- ► Your eyes from anticipating
- ► Your mouth from needing to be the first one with the answer

Imagine being welcomed and cheered for being the "no-frills" version of who you are

What changes or thoughts do you notice?

The Limiting Thought:

If only I could be someone else

Have you ever looked at others and wished your life could be like theirs? This wish, of course, presumes they have a life without pain, doubt, or struggle. Envy robs you of time you could spend enjoying your life.

Your life is the one you have here and now. This is the only body you ever get. This moment is the only span you get to play with.

You can reject your life or you can cherish it. You can live fully or you can postpone life…kind of. The challenge is that once the moment is past, it's gone. The more you accept the life you have right now, the more energy, possibility, safety, and sense of alignment you'll experience.

Being more connected to your life, exactly as it is, gives you greater possibility about what you might choose next.

One-Minute Transformation:

Welcome home

Pause. Settle. Open.

What if, for one minute, you allowed yourself to stop comparing yourself, your home, and your family to others?

- ► Allow yourself to mentally trace the boundaries of your skin.
- ► Breathe gently, filling up your entire body with more bubbles of oxygen.
- ► Hold the awareness of your entire being in your mind's eye.
- ► Feel yourself fully inhabiting this body.

Imagine meeting yourself at the door and welcoming him or her home to this unfinished, imperfect life.

What would be freed up if you fully inhabited your current life?

What do you particularly enjoy in your home?

The Limiting Thought:

Nothing can change this

Sometimes there are situations that seem to be rigidly unchangeable. That's when a concept from fine art provides a useful alternative.

In art composition, there is a concept called figure and ground. The figure is what the viewer focuses on, and the ground is everything else.

Similarly, when you have a problem you focus on it. Your problem is usually very clear and definite. It dominates your consciousness, especially how possible or impossible a solution seems.

In most cases, you don't even notice there is a ground or a bigger picture for your problem. However, the figure depends on the ground for its existence.

For example, think of a tree. Change the water, light, roots, soil, and you change the outcome for the tree. The opportunity for producing a different outcome or having a different experience of the situation is out there. You can change the figure starting with the ground.

One-Minute Transformation:

Change the ground

Pause. Settle. Open.

Close your eyes for a moment and imagine your problem as a character. *Give it shape, color, mass.*

Now, change your focus to explore the ground the problem exists in. *What's going on in the rest of the picture?*

- ► Change the color, season, or setting of the ground.
- ► Change the scale so the problem is tiny and everything else is huge.
- ► Put the problem somewhere incongruous, like stuck in a tree, in the blender, or in the middle of the highway.

How has your perception of your problem changed?

Where might there be opportunities to change things?

The Limiting Thought:

I'm a fraud

Many people believe that despite evidence to the contrary, they are imposters. No matter how much they have accomplished, they cannot fully internalize their competency. A cacophony of voices assails the afflicted—not smart enough, not perfect, just lucky, etc.

Perhaps you can identify.

Thoroughly addressing the syndrome is too big for the parameters of this book. At the same time, a book about limiting thoughts would be incomplete without mentioning it.

There is one aspect worth spending a minute on: In what ways does bearing the fraud banner serve you? Instead of trying to change it, embrace the idea that you need it as a safe haven, armor, bridge, or resistance, or for some other important function.

For one minute, listen to why you need it right now. The idea is not to change anything, rather to be able to support your deeper needs even more effectively.

One-Minute Transformation:

Hold Steady and Embrace

Pause. Settle. Open.

Give over to the experience of feeling like a fraud. Scan your body and mind to inventory the effects. Just name them without trying to fix or change anything—for example, "no substance... racing thoughts... tongue pushing against my teeth... really tight shoulders..." or other sensations.

Imagine that a pink cloud is forming over your head. It surrounds you in compassion. It is the perfect temperature and texture. It also provides the perfect kind of contact with your skin so that you can surrender to its support and acceptance. Allow yourself to just be, as you are right now, in your skin.

Before you open your eyes, listen to any message this experience has for you and find a place to keep the cloud so you have it handy, any time.

What message—in words or imagery—did you receive?

The Limiting Thought:

I just need more discipline

Big projects or changes often seem daunting. You find yourself unable to "get a handle on it." You berate yourself for lacking discipline, but that doesn't seem to have any effect on the outcome either.

There is a secret way to break the pattern: Do less.

Do so much less that you're able to use capillary action to draw you to success. Capillary action enables liquid to flow in opposition to the force of gravity. It happens at a molecular level as the molecules of the liquid are attracted to the molecules of its vessel.

Similarly, if you break down your task into tiny bits, it can start moving on its own. Instead of focusing on the end result, think of what the first step would be, then break that down by halves into smaller and smaller steps until movement to the next micro-step is almost undetectable and irresistible.

Once you have succeeded at breaking down your task into so many little grains, it's almost effortless to succeed as you accomplish one after the next and the next, until momentum accelerates you beyond the giant barriers of inertia.

One-Minute Transformation:

Use capillary action of change

Pause. Settle. Open.

Think of a project or change you want to make.

What is your idea of the first step?

What would half of your first step be? It could be half the complexity, effort, or goal, to name a few of the qualities you could parse.

Now cut that in half. What would that entail?

Continue cutting the size of the step in half until you'd need a special microscope to detect it. It's probably so small that by the time you've identified it, you've already done it.

What would your half steps be?

What would be the smallest step you might take?

The Limiting Thought:

This is the truth

You believe that what you perceive is the truth.

This is a natural and very useful function of our brain as it sifts all the stimuli coming into our organism and tells us how to respond. It's an evolution-tested process that helps you avoid running into literal and figurative walls, dress appropriately for weather, and earn good grades, among other things.

However, in your relationships, your quick and certain responses cause trouble. You assume that you know others' motives, and you jump to conclusions about their actions.

You make assumptions automatically. These assumptions become the basis of your beliefs. Your beliefs shape what, how, and when you see things, as well as what those things mean. The resulting combination is your version of reality.

We rarely question the assumptions at the foundation of our thoughts—even though we create them. But when you do challenge these assumptions, you'll discover different realities are possible.

One-Minute Transformation:

Assume that the opposite is true

Pause. Settle. Open.

You'll need paper and pen for this exercise. Think of a time when you felt someone wrongly judged, insulted, or ignored you. Write it across the top of the page.

Make two columns. On the left side, write down three assumptions you have about what their actions meant and what you thought this person was saying about you.

Now imagine that the opposite of each of your assumptions is true. Be willing to be unrealistic. Write each in the right side.

If these assumptions were true, how would that change your interpretation?

What might happen if the opposite of your assumption were true?

The Limiting Thought:

I don't want to hurt them

Do you say "yes" to things you don't really want to do? Do you tell yourself that you don't want to hurt someone's feelings or you want to appear to be a good friend?

You might think you're protecting the other person or doing something good by being disingenuous with them. Part of you probably believes that they will not be able to have a good time without you. Saying "yes" protects you from having to tell the other person what you want.

It takes a lot of courage for you to reveal your wants, but it's the most appropriate response. The root of courage is *coeur,* the French word for heart. When you're sharing your heart, you're in an authentic and satisfying relationship. Keeping another person in your heart means that you are neither "one up" nor "one down" from them; rather, you're "encouraging" each other.

One-Minute Transformation:

Activate courage

Pause. Settle. Open.

Think of a situation when you committed yourself with a disingenuous "yes."

First of all, forgive yourself. Take a few breaths, increasing your compassion.

As you increase your kindness, listen to and feel the pulse of your heart. Imagine that your heart can become bigger and that it has a voice that's becoming more distinct. What is your heart telling you right now?

Stay in this heart space and imagine the other person or situation in it with you as you continue to breathe. What would you really like to say to them? What would you really like to do with them?

What releases?

What opens up?

The Limiting Thought:

I don't dream

When you dream or muse, what is the range of options you allow? Ridiculous, far-flung, or fanciful? Practical? Those esteemed by others? Or something else? Are you concerned that your dreams are not the *right* dreams?

If so, you are choking off inspiration at the tap. If you have a lot of rules about what your dreams are supposed to be, you are discounting the ones that may be tugging on your sleeve.

It's like being in a richly diverse forest and seeing only a certain kind of tree. You need to notice more by paying attention to all the little drops of desire, springs of interest, and layers of life forms. Take your wild imaginings off the leash, so they can fuel "Why not?" or "How do I get more of that?" If you find yourself editing your own dreams, try the following transformation.

One-Minute Transformation:

Practice saying "yes"

Pause. Settle. Open.

Notice how "yes" feels.

Start by saying "yes" to yourself right now. Put aside all conditions, situations, prospects, reservations, and pressures. Just say "yes." Nod your head "yes" as you say it.

Think back to when you were a child. Ask yourself the following questions. As thoughts or memories emerge, just nod your head and say, "yes" to each one.

- ▶ What did you play in your imaginary world?
- ▶ What or who fascinated you?
- ▶ What was the most outrageous thing you ever dreamed?
- ▶ What would be just ten percent more daring?

As you go through the rest of the day, notice when you are criticizing yourself, and, instead think "yes!"

Notice how you feel acknowledging your dreams and passions.

The Limiting Thought:

It's hopeless

When you arrive at a moment of hopelessness, it feels bad, even dire. The urge to give up is almost irresistible. However, giving up is the easy way out. There is an alternative I learned while doing home-repair projects.

Dale, the hardware store cashier, said, "Every house project requires at least three trips to the store. No matter if I know exactly what I need or not. You get back to the project and discover that you're short or you are missing yet another piece. You just have to go back and forth, learning a little more about what you really need."

The same can be said of human experience. Instead of locking yourself out of an endeavor, you can go back to your metaphoric hardware store. You can get the next piece you know you'll need, and, perhaps, some new information about how to install it. Most importantly, you can embrace the reality that you'll most likely need yet another trip before you're done.

One-Minute Transformation:

Get the next piece

Pause. Settle. Open.

First, close your eyes and scan your body to find your place of hopelessness. Get very curious about what "the end" looks like to you; describe as many qualities and details as you can.

Acknowledge whatever you feel.

Ask your "end" if it is willing to consider another possibility. If the answer is "no," be willing to wait. If the answer is "yes," read on.

Since you have such a clear view of what the end looks like, imagine going to a hardware store and finding exactly the kind of patch, connector, or tow that would enable you to extend or revive your end.

What do you need to learn to make the piece adhere or work for you?

What does that new piece connect to?

The Limiting Thought:

I'm a failure

Improvisation teacher Matt Smith is the inventor of the *Failure Bow*. Since the only way to learn is to make the attempt, he asks, "What if, instead of being shamed, we were congratulated for our failures?"

In his class, each person makes a proud declaration: "I screwed up!" or "I did it again!" throwing their hands up in surrender. The rest of the class explodes in applause and cheers.

The impact of cheering my so-called mistakes was that I could release myself from the deep freeze of my shame and move on. With others, it freed me from my judgment of them and neutralized potential arguments.

This is such a profound experience, I'm committed to adding it to our practice of communication. It should be as universal a practice as shaking hands.

One-Minute Transformation:

Cheer your mistakes

Pause. Settle. Open.

Find a space where you can make a little noise.

Remember a mistake you made recently. Notice how simply applying a label, "I made a mistake," affects your breathing, the tension in your head and neck, and the quality of your thoughts.

Now imagine getting approval for taking whatever kind of step you took and getting the support you need to move on. Imagine a crowd applauding in approval as you declare, "I failed!" or "I did it again!"

If you are feeling really daring, request an audience and ask them to applaud enthusiastically. Say it out loud. Jump. Pump your arms up and take a bow.

What do you notice about how you think of your past now?

The Limiting Thought:

I have to do it for them

The experienced traveler will tell you that the most important thing you can do to prepare for a good trip is to leave most of your stuff behind.

When you sort the mental baggage you carry, there will be memories, knowledge, values, and skills that you'll want to retain. However, you also weigh yourself down with a lot of assumptions about what others expect and value. There are probably many times when you've sacrificed yourself because you believed you had to do it for someone else.

The interesting thing is when you actually ask the other person about their expectations, they often don't hold the same ones as you. For example, I've denied myself exercise, overspent on presents, and attended parties to prove that I deserved the host's friendship. But what I've learned was that they just like being around me and sharing an experience.

Setting down my bloated sense of what other people value took a huge weight off my shoulders and opened up the possibility of more fun.

One-Minute Transformation:

Lighten your load

Pause. Settle. Open.

Imagine yourself on your life journey, carrying all of your memories, beliefs, experiences, and treasures on your back in special packages. Imagine the weight and bulk of your load and how it influences the way you move.

For a moment, imagine setting everything down. How does it feel to take it off? What is on your manifest?

Which ones can you leave behind now?

Which ones are necessary to keep with you? Maybe there are some you neither want to abandon nor carry. What kind of storage would suit them?

Allow yourself to feel the newly lightened load.

How might you mark this spot in case you want to pick these things up?

What might life be like without the things you are leaving behind?

The Limiting Thought:

Oh, I'm not a _____

Listening to yourself, you may realize that you're defining yourself by what you are not: not really an artist, not organized, or simply just not enough. What day will you finally receive the certification that you are finally good enough?

Being good enough means that you can stop trying to compensate for imagined insufficiencies. You relax. You include yourself in groups without having a role to play. You allow yourself to receive support from the others, because you no longer have to continually prove something, nor push away their compliments because you believe they are not true.

Instead of defining yourself as not being something, try awarding yourself an honorary degree just for being exactly where you are.

One-Minute Transformation:

Today is the day

Pause. Settle. Open.

Take a series of four gentle breaths. Each time you inhale allow yourself to appreciate how your breath fills and enlivens you, exactly the way you are right now.

Today, you are receiving the National Medal of Sufficiency. It's official. You are Good Enough. You have arrived. There is nothing else to prove, no one's approval you need, nowhere better to be.

Notice the effects of this declaration.

What would you say if you started describing yourself in terms of all the great things that you are?

What might you start doing, now that you have received this certification?

The Limiting Thought:

Just in case...

"I'm done with that... I'm moving on," you say. However, do your closets tell a different story? Hidden from sight are clothes and files you keep "just in case" or "so I can keep the door open." While this seems like a good idea, it's also a way to avoid the discomfort of moving on.

When you think, "I'm keeping the door open," it really means that your attention is still focused on the past. "Just in case" means you are still lugging that "case" around. Moving on means ending it, completed exactly the way it is, not the way you wish it were.

Ending invites both mourning for what is lost and celebrating strengths built on a legacy that endures. Sometimes the ending calls for a hug, sometimes a wail—but it always involves a final punctuation mark. Then there is space for a new dream.

One-Minute Transformation:

End something

Pause. Settle. Open.

Allow your breath to pleasure you, just as you are right now.

Imagine you can zoom out, like an interactive map, so you can see yourself in the context of the rest of your life:

- ▶ What do you need to end?
- ▶ What needs to be honored, acknowledged, or mourned?

Allow one thing you are ready to release to come forward in your mind. Give it some focused attention. What needs to happen in order for you to release it?

Perhaps you can let it go like a helium balloon that floats away in the sky. Perhaps there are some steps. Notice what the first one is.

Allow yourself a moment to reintegrate and close this chapter.

What do you need to end?

The Limiting Thought:

I just have to break some bad habits

I was a compulsive eater for years. When I binged, I would be overwhelmed with guilt, shame, and despair. In spite of my best efforts to discipline and punish myself into "good" behavior, I couldn't break the vicious cycle: I overate, beat myself up, prayed for redemption… only to fail again the next time I passed a plate of cookies.

One key to freedom was embracing the "bad" behavior as my best effort to give myself comfort and approval. When I accepted that my intentions were positive, I could get under the surface and learn about the underlying dynamics. I could engage with the underlying needs in new ways.

For example, my eating and thought patterns were protective and effective. When I rejected myself, I never had to experience the ridicule I feared from others. When I ate, I never had to feel my fear of failure or reach out and ask for the love I needed in the moment.

One-Minute Transformation:

See the positive in the unacceptable

Pause. Settle. Open.

Think of a habit you wish you could change. Just for a minute, suspend your judgment that it should be any different from what it is.

During that minute:

- ► Accept that the habit aligns with your deeper needs.

- ► Increase your curiosity about what those needs are.

- ► Assume that your motivations are positive.

What are some positive intentions behind your habit?

Thank yourself for having such effective strategies in place. Appreciate the expertise you have developed in deploying this strategy. Just for a few moments, fully embrace this unacceptable trait.

What is your "bad habit" working so hard to do for you?

The Limiting Thought:

Maybe...

In spite of my best efforts, I've not figured out how to bi-locate. I can only do one thing with a given chunk of time. I have to make a decision about what gets done, which usually means giving something up or risking offending someone. And, yet, I fear just saying "no."

Perhaps you can identify?

An unambiguous "no" clears the path for a definite "yes."

Managing all the "maybes" or "ought tos" takes a ton of time and energy from everyone. Not only do you have an added burden, but it also puts added burden on the person inviting you. A "No thank you" clears mental space and empowers both parties to move on to getting what each of you wants.

A definite "no" frees everyone—especially you—to experience the excitement of "yes."

One-Minute Transformation:

Dare to say no

Pause. Settle. Open.

Think of all the options and commitments you are trying to manage. For a minute, assume there are no negative repercussions to saying no and that there is no "right" thing to do. What would you give up?

Imagine that the greatest gift you can give is a clear "no." Just for practice, say "no" out loud and shake your head. Repeat six to eight times.

Pause and notice any changes in your body, energy, and emotions when you say no.

What would you like to say no to?

What might you like to say yes to?

The Limiting Thought:

It's kryptonite

Superman was rendered powerless in the presence of the mythical material kryptonite.

Everyone has his or her own kryptonite. There are certain thoughts that, at times, I let diminish me; for example, I don't have children, or enough success. It's as if I turn on the vacuum cleaner and suck my entire self-worth out of me because of what I perceive as a blemish on my life.

You probably have your own version of kryptonite. What's important to remember is that a particular condition is just one aspect of who you are, a hugely complex being. The condition or the removal of the condition is no guarantee of happiness. More importantly, nobody is keeping score.

Re-inflate your self worth by increasing your awareness of your many and complex dimensions. Then you'll regain the power to pull the cord on your own worthiness vacuum. That act alone is an antidote. But you can do more; namely, keep noticing the many aspects of yourself that are continually creating a rich, fulfilling life.

One-Minute Transformation:

Revive yourself

Pause. Settle. Open.

Have some colored pencils and paper handy.

Close your eyes and feel your breath inflate your lungs. For the next three breaths, imagine you're pumping yourself up like a ball.

As you become more inflated, sense your whole life in 3D. Allow an image to come into your mind with specific colors, shapes, volumes, textures, patterns, and energy levels. Wait until it forms clearly in your mind.

Draw a picture or symbol of what you see.

Now think of something you believe you lack. Where does it fit in the picture of your whole life? Add it to your drawing.

What do you notice about the complexity of your life?

The Limiting Thought:

I'll just squeeze in one more thing

You probably never intend to be late. However, a few minutes before you have to leave, you think something like, "Oh, I can squeeze in one more thing..." The result is invariably a squeeze on you.

Instead of sanity, you brew the perfect stress storm. Since you are now racing to finish something, you get tense. Then you rely on the highly unlikely alignment of the planets for no traffic, a convenient place to park, or to provide all the materials you'll need. You stop breathing. Your thoughts are racing and filled with apologies, excuses, and self-recrimination.

You sacrifice access to your best thinking, increase tension, and trigger low self-esteem... quite a price to pay for "one more thing."

It sounds simple and makes a lot of sense to do one less thing, but doing it is like giving up an addiction. This is practice as an act of supreme courage. You have to dare to waste a little time and risk not being "productive."

One-Minute Transformation:

Dare to do less

Pause. Settle. Open.

Do less for one minute. Here's how:

- ▸ Sit in your chair. However you are sitting, imagine that you can sink into the chair just a little more.

- ▸ Scan your body. Wherever you notice tension, imagine you can release it just a little.

- ▸ Notice your thoughts. Whatever qualities they have, such as fast/slow, harsh/soft, berating/supportive, and whatever activities you are occupied with, such as making lists, comparing, or replaying, invite yourself to think a little less.

- ▸ For a few breaths, soak in the effects of the exercise.

What are the effects of deliberately doing less?

What might happen if you made a point to do just a little less for a whole day?

The Limiting Thought

If only I were _____

Does loving yourself depend on meeting criteria like the right job, fitness, mate, weight, appearance, etc?

If you're like me, you spend a lot of time trying to get it right or punishing yourself when you miss the mark. You think you need to be something and someone different from who you are today.

In fact, holding onto your criteria will have the opposite effects from what you imagine: Instead of leading you to more love, they will drive you further into self-loathing. They will prevent you from receiving the love your environment is abundantly providing.

There is no "better" way to be. Even if you had more money or beauty and the perfect mate, you would still be you. The richer or more beautiful version of you would find new flaws, setting the cycle of postponing love in motion, again. Instead, what if you stopped improving and just enjoyed yourself, starting now?

One-Minute Transformation:

Embrace your whole self now

Pause. Settle. Open.

Observe your breath carefully. With each inhalation, imagine the air filling your body with carbonation. Imagine that these bubbles are delivering a little hug of more oxygen to your cells, so that your entire being is held in a bubbly embrace.

As you exhale, imagine that just as gently, you can release one of the conditions you've placed on yourself for being lovable.

Gently imagine that your condition dissolves with your exhalation. For one minute, allow yourself to accept exactly who you are right now.

If there is some reason you cannot let go, allow the carbonation to surround your area of hurt until it floats, tenderly supported.

Notice the effects of increased acceptance.

The Limiting Thought:

No way!

Sometimes you may feel utterly lost and unable to do anything to find your way to a better place. During those moments you probably don't want advice.

What might be more helpful is a metaphor or story to open up the gates of possibility and community. Metaphor or imagery is like oil that gets the machinery of your creative brain moving again.

Metaphor seeps into cracks and crevices, illuminating deeper secrets and opening up layers of emotional concrete. There are many poems that use metaphor and are easy to understand and identify with. It's not about the right poem; rather, it's about the one that speaks to you.

Poetry reminds you that you're not alone on this journey of being human.

One-Minute Transformation:

Read a poem out loud

Pause. Settle. Open.

If you aren't a poetry reader, it may feel like a big stretch to embrace a poem, let alone to read the words out loud. However, the out loud part is an important aspect.

You can start by singing "Row, Row, Row Your Boat" four or five times.

Here are a few of my favorite poems (you can find the full text online.) Yours may be in a different language or have a different tone. Or maybe it's your own poetry that needs to be spoken out loud.

> *Love After Love* by Derek Walcott
>
> *The Journey* by Mary Oliver
>
> *I Dwell in Possibility* by Emily Dickinson
>
> *The Peace of Wild Things* by Wendell Berry

Read so you let the words sink in.

What is the poem saying to you?

What are the effects of reading out loud for you?

Chapter 5

An Owner's Manual

Frequently asked questions

You have sampled the *NextU* tools and techniques. But perhaps you have some lingering questions or challenges in applying them. Here are some of the most common questions:

When you say, "Notice the effects," what am I supposed to notice?

What if I tried it, but didn't feel anything?

What if I don't like the feeling I get?

Just tell me what the right way is.

Isn't this just positive thinking?

How do I really change? (I still criticize myself, overeat, compulsively shop, etc.)

What if my situation or thoughts don't show up in the book?

What if my family doesn't like the way I'm changing?

*What is the best way to apply **NextU** with a friend?*

How can I begin if I can't separate out a single thought or experience?

In what ways are these exercises applicable during a life crisis?

My situation is too complicated. How can I start?

I'm too busy as it is. Why should I take more time to do these?

What's so great about being in the now?

When you say, "Notice the effects," what am I supposed to notice?

This instruction is deliberately ambiguous. It's an invitation for you to expand your awareness to your whole being, environment, and psyche. You might focus deeply within or expand beyond your current boundaries.

If that's still too vague, here are a few specific questions you can ask yourself to help guide your focus:

▸ Physically: What is my degree of relaxation or tension in my skin, muscles, eyes, or brain?

▸ Presence: How has my comfort or safety in being exactly who or where I am changed?

▸ Emotionally: Am I calmer? Do I feel more relaxed? Or am I more agitated?

- ▶ Breath: Am I breathing more easily or less? Did it feel good to take a breath?

- ▶ Sense of possibility: Do I have a spark of hope? A different perspective or horizon? Renewed optimism? Awareness of limitation?

- ▶ Other shifts to note: Am I able to think of something other than the thought that drove me to practice?

What if I tried it, but didn't feel anything?

This kind of work may be new for you. If so, be patient and curious. To a large degree you look for the results you expect to get. These sensations may be outside of the spectrum of feelings that you're used to responding to in your day-to-day life. Ask yourself, "What else might I be experiencing?" Look for changes in your physical body, the quality of your thoughts, tension in your muscles, expansion in your range of vision or hearing. Tiny, even micro, changes are significant.

What if I don't like the feeling I get?

Asking yourself to become quiet for a minute can be anxiety-provoking and uncomfortable. The effort may seem stupid, pointless, or irritating. These are natural defensive reactions by your logical brain.

When something is new, it is by definition unfamiliar. For example, think about what happened the last time you tried to get a young child to try a new food. If something is beyond the comfort zone of familiarity, it's easy to label it as *bad*. When something has a moral overlay, you react by thinking that it's imperative to get rid of it.

You might experiment with reframing. Look at your feeling and these exercises as a scientific experiment. In science, something unfamiliar is an invitation to explore without prejudice, instead of rejecting it out of hand. Doing this you invite yourself to tolerate the feeling just a little more.

Other feelings—sadness, rage, fear, or longing—that seem scary or seem like they belong to places you'd rather not go may trigger an alarming sense of a loss of control. Remember, you're always in control. You choose how deeply or peripherally you want to feel something. At the same time, if you recognize a big issue, get help. That is what therapists are for.

If you can, inhibit your immediate reaction of fight or flight and try to tolerate the feelings. Remind yourself that you're safe. By feeling more, you're expanding the spectrum of understanding yourself, so in reality you're expanding your control. In addition, you might think of other experiences in life where you gave up a little control by trying something new and got more pleasure in return, like first discovering salted caramel ice cream or massages.

Just tell me what the right way is.

If you've been very successful at accomplishing things, you'll be looking for the "right way" to do these exercises. But the only right way is the way that provides more ease, clarity, energy, safety, or wholeness. Instead of intellectually deriving what is right, you need to allow for ambiguity so you can feel your answer.

If you're worried that you're not succeeding or are thinking that you're not "doing it right," you might notice that you have some judgment about what success is. (This is a perfect opportunity to practice a *NextU* intervention.)

Try reframing your evaluation. Consider:

- ▶ What if I'm doing this exactly right?

- ▶ What if I dropped my expectations?

- ▶ What if my experience contains the perfect response?

- ▶ How did this help me see or feel something different?

Isn't this just positive thinking?

NextU is quite different from techniques that tell you to just replace negative thoughts with positive thoughts in three main ways: the role the thoughts play, the mind-body approach, and how you assess success. Instead of positive thinking, *NextU* is about positive being.

There is an assumption in the positive-thinking industry that negative thoughts are bad and to be extinguished. I propose in *NextU* that thoughts are valuable signals that something needs attention. When you neutralize the judgments expressed in a thought, you can see them as symptoms of comfort or pain and find ways to realign.

Your body's systems are built from wisdom on how to thrive. This is a wisdom accumulated over billions of years of experimentation and adaptation. The *NextU* method gives you more tools to tap into and translate that natural sophistication and elegance. At times, the results you get may be subtle; other times, they will be loud and clear.

The first place you should look for results is in how your body feels. Instead of just trying to memorize a "right" answer, *NextU* helps you inhabit different possibilities that are created for and by you, which means you can recreate it whenever you need to. Whenever you have a felt experience of life, you have the evidence of being fully in the moment.

How do I really change?

I still criticize myself, overeat, shop compulsively, etc.
Behavior is the tip of an iceberg made from a hugely complex set of pre-existing conditions, experiences, patterns, relationships, decisions, beliefs, and assumptions. Your behavior is the visible portion of your beliefs, attitudes, and strategies for survival developed long ago. You may want professional therapy to help you untangle them and establish new habits. The *NextU* exercises are a great accompaniment to therapy.

You might increase your ability to notice change in yourself by changing where you look for results. In other words, you may be expecting a big problem to crumble. Instead of launching a frontal attack, try approaching it from the back or perhaps changing how you hold the problem in your body. Try to appreciate for one minute how you could have a new experience, or a different feeling or strategy. These exercises are meant to work on you more like the trickle of water over a stone than a blast from a fire hose. Sometimes seeping water wears down the stone; sometimes it works its way into the cracks, freezes, and splits the rock open.

Another barrier to change might be not being honest. A big or chronic problem could be present in your life because it works for you to have it. There are many reinforcing systems that keep it in place. It's not going to budge until it's safe enough for all those other systems to release a little.

What if my situation or thoughts don't show up in the book?

This book is not comprehensive; rather, it presents a slice of my personal view of the world. I'd love to hear what your situation is. Please contact me at ***nextu@mynextu**.com*.

You may or may not find an exact match for your issue. These limiting thoughts arise from some pretty basic feelings that humans have used to make themselves miserable: shame, blame, comparison, doubt, fear, longing, despair, regret, etc. Even if you don't suffer from these emotions, you can still amplify your experiences of the "good stuff" through these practices.

What if my family doesn't like the way I'm changing?

Balancing the needs of a family with your own needs, especially if there is a job involved, is a delicate process. But all too often, people try to remove their own needs from the equation. Remember, family includes you: It's up to the entire family to find ways to accommodate the needs of all its members. Everyone needs to work collaboratively to make a family work.

What is the best way to do this with a friend?

Often having another person pay attention makes it easier to stay focused. A partner can free you to focus on your own experience more fully. Each of you can act as a guide for one another, reading the directions out loud and providing silent pauses at the appropriate moments to breathe and reflect.

A few agreements will lead to a richer experience for both of you:

▶ Respect your partner. You might discuss how each of you will know you're being respected.

▶ Don't offer any evaluation or interpretation of your partner's experience. Inhibit your desire to fix the other's experience or problem.

▶ Remain silent at the end of the exercise until the partner doing the exercise is ready to talk, which might take another minute or two.

▶ Trade roles so that both of you experience the exercise before talking about your own experience.

▶ Include time for both of you to reflect on the experience. You may want to talk or write or draw. Pick the form that works best for you and be aware that your partner may want something different.

How can I begin if I can't separate out a single thought or experience?

If you have a jumble of thoughts, it's usually due to a couple of things. You're upset about something, have competing priorities, or your thoughts are racing too fast. It could be any one or a combination of these reasons.

If it's because you're upset, first acknowledge that you're upset. Some big emotion is dominant and needs attention first before you can think. Visualize getting a hug from someone much bigger than you that lasts for as long as you need. When you're ready, imagine that person stepping away. The calming process has already started, so continue by slowing down and walking through the foundation practices outlined in Chapter 3: pause, settle, and open.

If new waves of upset feelings well up in you, start over. It may be you're not ready to do anything other than be overwhelmed right now. If you are ready, it's likely that you will notice that one thought has become a refrain or you'll notice that what you need is a particular exercise that focuses on intervention, inspiration, or breakthrough. Then you can select your exercise accordingly.

Competing priorities also show up as jumbled thoughts. Deliberately slow down. A thorough how-to guide on slowing down is part of the foundation discussion in Chapter 3. A shortcut is to pay close attention to your breathing, relax your muscles, and soften your eyes and tongue. Play the referee to your own thoughts; listen to and document all sides. Once you see the list of your thoughts, you can pick one for further investigation.

If your thoughts are racing, the directions above also apply. Racing thoughts are a symptom of feeling like you're in an emergency. You need to feel safe physically first. Then you can intentionally slow down your breath and body. Alternatively, do aerobic physical exercise that makes you breathe hard for at least a half an hour, and then assess your readiness to identify a thought you want to work with.

In what ways are these applicable to life crises?

First aid for your mental and emotional self is not much different from what is called for to attend to your physical body. First, metaphorically, stop the mental or emotional bleeding and get out of danger. Before any rescue team goes into an avalanche or earthquake zone, they wait for the situation to stabilize. **NextU** is not a substitute for or equivalent to professional help, but it can support and enhance that process by helping you stabilize before seeking other help. Once you're safe, you'll naturally start thinking about what might be next.

NextU practices can help show your emotional, nervous, hormonal, muscular, and limbic systems how you can move out of catastrophe. The more you get into your body, the broader and deeper your foundation of resilience becomes.

► Ground yourself (see the foundations discussion in Chapter 3). Get connected to this moment, location, and yourself, right now.

► Intervene on catastrophe thinking. It's easy for your mind to run away with disaster scenarios. Stop it. They're not helpful. Come back to this moment, this place, and this body.

► Breathe consciously, meaning focus your attention on the entire process of inhaling and exhaling. Notice what moves or changes in response to your breath. Notice the sensation of the air coming into your nostrils and leaving. Notice how much of your lungs you're employing and if your diaphragm is moving.

If you start to feel dizzy, let go of the breathing practice and put your head down between your knees. This may be a sign that you're not exhaling enough or that you need to soften your breath.

Stop this practice if you become more agitated. Continue if it creates more comfort or space.

An alternative breathing practice is to drape your belly over an exercise ball. Inhale as if you are breathing into the ball. Allow yourself to feel the ball pressing back on the exhalation. Stay there as long as it feels calming.

▶ Cry. Wail. Scream. If you're worried about noise, put an empty bucket or waste paper basket over your head. It's amazing how therapeutic making a big noise is.

▶ Signal to your nervous system to turn off its emergency alarm by asking someone to hold you, or by swaddling yourself. You may have witnessed how effectively wrapping a baby snugly calms the baby. That signaling response does not vanish just because we have matured.

▶ Get into a bath, a hot tub, or other body of water to reintegrate. This is another primal soothing technique, reminiscent of the womb and our ancient connection to the seas.

▶ If you're in crisis because of someone else's need, remember to "put on your own oxygen mask first." You cannot help anyone else if you're in pieces yourself.

My situation is too complicated. How can I start?

If you view your situation as too complicated, you can try to single out individual threads or you may need to hold steady exactly where you are.

▶ If you're feeling scattered, focus on the foundations practices in Chapter 3. Once you're anchored to your body and able to pay attention to the present moment, you can deal with the next dominant thought.

▶ Sometimes you're not ready to change. You may have a long list of everything that is wrong, yet no suggestion that anyone gives is welcome. "Saming," staying the same, is a very underrated decision.

▶ If several thoughts appeal to you, pick one; the order in which you address them doesn't matter. But make sure you take time to notice and integrate the effects of each exercise discretely. One may work better for you and be worth repeating.

▶ Play. Follow your instincts. If you notice one of your limiting thoughts is missing from my list, please contact me. Together we can help address how to transition away from it. Then we can make it available to others in the same situation.

I'm too busy as it is. Why should I take more time to do these?

You are busy—perhaps crazy busy. How often have you thought, "What happened to this day," or week, month, or season? You may have a sense that life's racing by, while your intentions to have an abundant garden, be the person who bakes cookies and delivers them to families experiencing stress, send birthday cards, or get more sleep are gathering dust in a heap by the front door. Yet, time is your most valuable and limited resource.

Consider this: How much of your life do you actually own? How much do you give up to do things you don't even care about? Take out your calendar or your checkbook and review how often your core values show up. It's often a revelation. Besides serving as on-the-spot first aid, these exercises are a core-values-fitness program, increasing your connection to what really matters to you and how to get more of those things into your life.

What is so great about being in the now?

You cannot go back and change the past, nor can you live in the future. Even if you agree with this premise, chances are the past and the future are where the stream of your thoughts tends to flow. Your mind is preoccupied with the past and the future. Yet the past and future is not now.

Now is when all great stuff happens. Now holds your peak experiences. Now is when you experience authenticity, integrity, love, wonder, and your other core values. It measures your life in terms of "being," as opposed to "accomplishing."

What other questions do you have?

Please share your questions on the *NextU* Facebook page or email me at *nextu@mynextu.com*. Your questions are likely shared by others and will enrich the whole community.

Additionally, you can find more helpful resources with an Internet search, from your local librarian or pastor, priest, imam, or rabbi. Any of these sources can direct you to many volumes of great writing, wonderful teachers to study with, and practices you can adopt within every spiritual tradition

Conclusion

Now you have a wide variety of ways to change your perception of the moment and enjoy your life more. You can freshen your curiosity, intervene on your internal bullying, and get out from under the weight of your expectations. When challenges knock you down, you now have new ways to find the inspiration, intervention, or breakthrough you need to recover.

Instead of mindlessly repeating the same vicious cycle, you can use the *NextU* practices to become the person you most want to be in that moment. You get to *be* your next you. That version of you has the peace of mind to free yourself from the burdens of the past and anticipation of the future; that next you has confidence in your own answers and the courage to step into the great unknown of what might be possible.

The minute or two you spend with a *NextU* exercise gives you highly effective leverage points you can use to transform your life and learn to own it. In this context, owning it means that you inhabit your present moment more fully. It means that you can infuse any moment of life with the joy, appreciation, wonder, or connection that you formerly reserved for select peak experiences.

Now what?

If life is a journey, you now have the guide to lead you through many different kinds of treacherous terrain and inclement weather conditions that slow you down, deflate your tires, mire you in muck, and prevent you from seeing and acting on all the possibilities ahead. Popular wisdom (also known as the first page of Google results) says that your brain produces between 12,000 and 70,000 thoughts per day. Obviously, this collection of limiting thoughts represent just a tiny sample of all that you think.

By now, you know there is a way to choosing more ease, comfort, and connection:

- ► Put your life on pause for a minute.

- ► Breathe more.

- ► Increase your receptivity to what is going on in your whole system.

- ► Reframe, increase compassion, and risk something different.

- ► Allow yourself to experience whatever feelings arise without judgment.

What would you do if the entire energy of the universe were focused on liberating your energy, curiosity, and delight?

NextU invites you to entertain this provocative question by granting yourself one whole minute of your life free from habitual patterns. You will find new resources of energy, pleasure, and daring that will fuel your decisions and awaken your awareness.

This is just the beginning. I'm entrusting this handful

of seeds with the potential for greater aliveness to you so that your life may flower.

The back story about why I wrote this book

On my thirtieth birthday I sat in my friend Sherry's kitchen and declared, "My life is too excruciatingly painful. If this is the way it's going to be, I'm going to commit suicide. If you go to my funeral and hear people say, '*How could this have happened? She was so happy. She had such a great smile,*' I want someone to know that there were real reasons that I couldn't go on."

My friend immediately took me to a therapist who inspired enough belief in me that things could be different that I was able to choose and persist on a path of healing. This was the beginning of My Big Recovery.

I became healthier, happier, and more whole, but fear, uncertainty, and doubt still stymied me. New life challenges continually showed up that knocked me off my equilibrium. I reacted by contracting back to my small, paralyzed, frightened self, like a snail curling back into its shell. When I was contracted mentally, emotionally, or physically, I had no sense anything else was possible. It was not enough to think positively. I had to feel something as well. I learned to pay attention to what helped me expand again to more possibility and aliveness.

So I continued my therapy, studies, and practices because aliveness had become so compelling. I became something of a junkie, wanting more of that wondrous, energized innocence, more of that connection and transcendence that I experienced in therapy. I developed the tools in this book as a way to come back to vibrant, expansive, infinitely possible aliveness, rather than contracting in on myself.

I got a master's degree in organizational leadership and completed a post-graduate fellowship focusing on facilitating group development. This work helped me understand how others learn and what individuals need to exercise self-leadership and do their great work in the world. I launched a coaching and consulting practice to share these insights with individuals and organizations.

I realized that many others, perhaps including you, shared the same diseases and afflictions I suffered from. We all need ordinary recoveries and ways to get us from wherever we find ourselves back across the puddle or crevasse of despair to the confidence, calm, and courage we need to see the possibilities before us.

Inspiration for the entrepreneur

Creativity is making something that didn't exist before. It's not limited to painting, performing, or other activities geared toward museums and theaters. It's about the emergence of an idea, expression, or solution that is not formulaic. Creativity is what I call on to solve the moment-to-moment challenges of life, and it results in something that is genuinely mine.

The ability to create requires continual, renewed courage, persistence, and trust as each instance requires something just a little different. These qualities are fragile, which is why I need resilience. As an entrepreneur, I have to pick myself up off the floor, metaphorically speaking, after moments of disappointment and doubt when positive feedback is lacking. I have to find encouragement to keep going, many times a day. I have to be willing to overcome blocks, become playful, see from a different perspective, unsnarl a massive tangle of negative thoughts, and try again to risk something new.

Let being be enough

I use the exercises in this book over and over every day. I need them to restore my courage, persistence, and trust. I need them to help me break through my procrastination and resistance when I would rather avoid everything. For example, I use these exercises dozens of times every time I sit down to write or edit.

I use these exercises when I experience impatience with the pace of change. I know that short of cutting off a leg, I won't loose thirty pounds in an hour. Or that in spite of my wishing, my fairy godmother will not show up to wave her magic wand nor will I be visited by a guru who will transmit instant enlightenment. However, I learned that I could change the way I experienced my body or my satisfaction with my life exactly the way it is. I realized I didn't have to change everything; I only need to change how I experience just one moment.

I spent a lot of time trying to be incredible. It was exhausting, and I almost always missed the mark. I was afraid to give up that standard, but I discovered that the more I let myself be a mere mortal, even a kind of ordinary, blundering human being, the more comfortable I was in my own skin. I noticed that the more I allowed my life to be ordinary, the more extraordinary it became, precisely because it was—and is—my life.

I spent years thinking that some day my prince would awaken me and, finally, I would get to live happily ever after. What I awakened to was the reality that I was wasting the life

I actually had and that I'd better start embracing it before it was over. As I inhabited my actual life, I needed a different kind of fuel than the hype, competition, and distortion I had previously driven myself with.

I needed to regularly fill up on the easy breathing that comes with optimism, learning, and curiosity. I needed to see that old strategies and stories no longer worked, and I needed to have the ability to release them. If I want a different experience of life, I have to be able to comprehend it by having a different perception of the world. Satisfying these needs requires doses of compassion, humor, and wonder.

Wow! I want more of that...

What was your last transcendent moment? Perhaps it was seeing a particular sunset or sunrise or work of art. Perhaps it was the flood of feeling good after vigorous exercise or a great kiss. Perhaps it was the clarity after a meditation retreat or the thrill of a roller-coaster ride. Whatever it was, these experiences leave you thinking, "Wow! I want more of that."

"More of that" is the potential of every moment. It's a matter of where you're looking and your receptivity to experiencing it. That is what these exercises will help you do—get more of that.

In short, I learned how to get from where I was feeling stuck to living with confidence, calm, courage, and so much more. I know can you, too. It's my sincere wish that this book gives you the nudge or support you need to remember the miracle you are.

What's your NEXT step with Posy Gering?

Posy's work catalyzes profound shifts that reveal new possibilities. Her speaking programs, written works, meeting facilitation, workshops and coaching sessions enable individuals and groups to address their most pressing challenges and act on their greatest opportunities.

Discover how she will serve you or your organization:
nextu@mynextu.com
(206) 769-9465

Get more of these easy steps to enjoy life more at
http://www.mynextu.com/contact/.

Acknowledgments

Although I get the byline on this book, it would never exist without the generosity and talent of many others.

I always wanted to write books, but that was before I knew what the work of creating one entailed. I was in love with the romance of being an author and having the rest of the world hang on my every thought. I had lists of book ideas. It only took forty years to start writing one.

Now, chastened by the blast furnace that clarifying and articulating ideas makes you go through, I know the author has something to do with the words. But the life of a book happens in the anonymous spaces in between the words and in the turning of the pages. The blank spaces are symbolic of the critical support roles of others. I am so humbly grateful for my supporters' selfless contributions and training in how to be a writer.

A few of the huge community I owe thanks to includes Ashisha, Luisa Simone, Andrea Driessen, Dianne Platner, Lea McLeod, Sonja Carson, Judy Peterson, Kathy Boullin, Kathy Humphrey, and Jessica Prince. No ask was too big. Their attention, gentle nudges, clear-sighted feedback, meals, walks, and unending support kept me moving forward.

I am so grateful for my editors: Judith Dern, Millie Loeb, Eleanor Licata, and Nancy Goll and designers Leslie Waltzer and Kristi Ryder who briskly shook out the manuscript, found the structure, slashed needless words and made sentences sparkle in return. I am humbly grateful to the friends who, via social media, responded immediately with authority and preferences about punctuation and grammar, title, cover, design and anything else.

Beyond the current care circle, I want to acknowledge a few who set my foundation, offered their shoulders to stand upon, and gave me the skill to build upon their great works. Remy Charlip, Shirley Kaplan, Burt Supree, and June Ekman, beloved teachers at Sarah Lawrence College, taught me the practical techniques of making things up and shared their lives in the arts. June mentored me through recovery, witnessed as I recreated my life and taught me many of the techniques I have adapted.

An Organization Systems Renewal (OSR) MA in Organizational Leadership gave me the courage and clarity to stand in my passion. The program provided understanding about the nature of beliefs and perception, models for change and how to design content—along with an amazing learning community.

Mitch Singer, the latest in a line of amazing Orgonomists, still teaches me the skill of resilience and the art of the felt experience of life. He guides me to start again, practice innocence, stay the course, redefine success, stay with experience longer, and recover faster.

And deep gratitude to everyone I told I was writing a book who responded with the belief that, of course, I could do it and deliver something they, personally, would be interested in reading.

Index of Exercises